HOW TO WIN OVER EMOTIONS

BY
J. J. TURNER, D. Min.

QUALITY PUBLICATIONS
P.O. BOX 1060
ABILENE, TEXAS 79604

By

J. J. Turner

ISBN:0-89137-315-2

DEDICATION

To **Isabel**, my loving wife and helper.
And to **Sandra**, my daughter and friend.
And to **John Alan**, my son and motivator.

TABLE OF CONTENTS

PREFACE

This morning, as I was thinking about writing this preface, two articles in the newspaper reminded me once again of the relevancy of this book. The captions on the articles were: "Stress Is Linked To Cancer" and "Exercise May Shield Against Heart Attack" (The Register, November 17, 1982, pp. D1, A14). Stress and exercise are two of the subjects covered in this book.

Life in our day is characterized as "Life in the fast-lane." Our theme song is Rush, Rush Rush. A popular book entitled *When I Relax I Feel Guilty* describes how millions feel in our society. They are uptight, or on the verge of an emotional explosion. Man seems to be able to control everything but himself.

Christians are not exempt from the runaway havoc of uncontrolled emotions. They have their share of anger, fear, depression, guilt, low self-esteem, and other emotional problems. This is true in spite of the fact that Christ came so that we may have abundant life and peace.

This book presents a Biblical approach to winning over emotions. It sets forth practical and usable suggestions for thinking and acting right. It is based upon the belief that God, through His Word, has given us all things that pertain to life and godliness (cf. II Peter 1:3). Every member of the church will benefit from this study.

This book is the outgrowth of a series of sermons I preached at the Newland Street church of Christ, Garden Grove, California. The material is arranged for personal as well as classroom study. There are questions at the end of each chapter to facilitate classroom participation. The teacher of this material, as well as the student, is encouraged to supplement it with his own research, questions and illustrations. God bless you in your quest to become more like our Savior. THE BEST IS YET TO BE! (I Corinthians 15:58).

J. J. Turner, D. Min.
Garden Grove, CA
November 17, 1982

TIPS FOR USING THIS BOOK IN CLASS STUDY

This book is designed to be studied. It may be studied on a personal basis or in a class situation. If you plan to use it in a class situation, I would suggest the following things to help you have the best possible class.

1. Be sure each member of the class has a copy of this book.
2. Encourage each member to read and study a chapter before you cover it in class.
3. As the teacher, find some good illustrations for some of the major points in each lesson. Encourage each member of the class to do likewise.
4. Teach the material in your own words.
5. Go over the "For Thought and Discussion" section in class. Encourage members of the class to bring written answers to class.
6. Prepare your own set of questions over the material, etc.
7. Allow the class time to discuss major points.
8. Be sure to encourage personal application of the material before you leave each class.
9. You may begin each class by asking the members to share how they have used the material studied in the last class (during the week).
10. Find additional verses of scripture for the lesson.
11. If time permits allow group work (e.g. getting into smaller groups for discussion and application, etc.: "Here is how I can use this point", "Here is what this means to me".)
12. Be creative.
13. Recommend reading in other books on certain subjects covered in a lesson.
14. Pray for wisdom (cf. James 1:5).
15. Consider inviting a guest to come and share with the class in an area he has special training or knowledge in (e.g., physician, counselor, etc.).

TIPS FOR USING THIS BOOK IN CLASS

CHAPTER ONE

MAN: AN EMOTIONAL BEING

"Rejoice with those who rejoice; mourn with those who mourn" (Romans 12:15).

INTRODUCTION

- "I don't know what happened to me, I just came apart when my husband made fun of my new dress. He made me so mad!"
- "When I hear 'God Bless America' tears come into my eyes."
- "I grew up in a home where it wasn't manly to cry."
- "He never gets emotional. A bomb couldn't move him."
- "She gives me a pain in the neck."

These five statements remind us of the emotional nature of man. Out of all of God's creation, he is unique. He has feelings and emotions which animals don't have. He can feel sad, glad, sorrow, joy, happiness, anger, fear, enthusiasm and a host of other emotions within the span of a few hours.

Contrary to the thinking of some persons in our day, I believe feelings play a very important role in man's everyday life. Without emotions a person becomes unnatural and callous within his heart. God created man with the ability to feel. Paul tells the Romans that God gave up the Gentiles because their emotions became vile (cf. Romans 1:26).

The challenge for man is to recognize the valid place for good, healthy emotions in his life. Likewise, he must realize how destructive negative and wrong emotions can be to his well being. He must control his emotions, which is possible through help from God. The Bible makes it very clear that some emotions are harmful, as well as sinful.

DEFINITION OF EMOTION

All of us know what an emotion is but very few can give a good definition of the term. How would you define it? Let's take a few minutes and see how others have defined emotion.

Dr. Clyde Narramore defines it as: "A mental state characterized by strong feelings such as fear, anger, love or hate."

Webster defines it as a: "Strong feeling; any specific feeling, a love, hate, fear, anger, etc."

The *Dictionary of Psychology* defines feeling as: "An elementary mental process which differs from sensation and which has dimension of pleasantness or unpleasantness."

The Oxford Dictionary of English Etymology defines emotion as: "physical disturbance; disturbance of mind or feeling; affection of the mind, feeling."

In his book *Pattern and Growth in Personality*, G. Allport defines emotion as: "the subjective coloring of motives, especially of motives that are thrown into conflict, or that make sudden or unexpected progress toward their goal."

Aristotle wrote: "By . . . the emotions, are meant those states which are attended by pain and pleasure, and which, as they change, make a difference in our judgments of the same thing."

"Emotion is an aroused 'feeling state' that accompanies an unusual degree of motivation," wrote Wayne C. Minnick.

When we look at the root word emotion in the Latin it is a compound of *e* (out of) and *movere* (to move), and suggests we move out of rest. Leander Keyser classifies emotions as: 1) sentient–corresponding to sense of perception; 2) intutional–immediate perception of reality, and 3) psychical–connected with understanding.

The Biblical writers use the words "heart" (*kardia*) and "bowels" (*splagchnon*) to express the emotions of man (cf. Matthew 22:37; I John 3:17; II Corinthians 2:4; Philippians 1:8). God created man with the ability to feel and be emotional. The challenge, however, is to understand the nature of our emotions and bring them under proper control.

Emotion is the product of what the mind thinks. It doesn't matter whether the mind knows if a statement or event is true or not, it will produce emotions in harmony with its thinking about it. This fundamental truth must never be forgotten: MAN PRODUCES HIS OWN EMOTIONS. This is hard to accept because we have been conditioned to blame others for our emotions and conduct. The person who said, "He made me mad," didn't understand this basic fact. A person produces his own anger within his mind, just as he produces his own happiness within himself. Emotion, therefore, is a feeling produced by thoughts held in the mind. Our thoughts shake us out of our peaceful condition into an emotional state.

THE POWER OF NEGATIVE EMOTION

A number of years ago, Elvis Presley sang a song which contained the phrase: "I'm all shook up." This was his way of saying, "I am very emotional." When we get emotional we get "shook up." The heart beats faster, the eyes bulge, the hands shake, the face turns pale or red, the voice crackles, the throat gets dry, the palms sweat, the eyes water, the face draws, and a host of other things occur (not all at the same time) when we get emotional. Emotions range from mild to severe. Some are easy to control; some are difficult to handle.

God has so made the body that all right emotions, right thoughts, and right attitudes produce right effects in the body. The British Medical Association is on record as saying that there is not a single cell in the body totally removed from the influence of the mind and emotion. Thus, the attitudes we hold in our minds produce emotions, which pass over into definite physical effects. Wrong thinking produces wrong emotions which produce wrong actions in our lives. This means, therefore, that we can change our lives through changing our thinking.

The effects of emotions upon the body are staggering. We turn "pale with fear," we "blush with embarrasment," we get "green with envy," we "shake with excitement," etc. We self-talk ourselves into all kinds of emotions. We say, "I don't like it," or "I feel ill when I think about it." Such thinking usually produces negative results. "She burns me up" is literally true. You hate her, and that hate burns you physically. The emotional triggers the physical. "He's a pill" – hard to swallow. "They drive me nuts" – they upset your mentality.

Dr. S. I. McMillen in his book *None of These Diseases* states: "Peace does not come in capsules! This is regrettable because medical science recognizes that emotions such as fear, envy, resentment and hatred are responsible for the majority of our sicknesses. Estimates vary from 60 percent to nearly 100 percent."

A business man saw a friend drop dead on a playing field. It scared him. His fear upset his own heart. He stayed home afraid to go to work for fear it would be too great a strain upon his own heart. He would go periodically to a doctor to be examined. In the strength of assurance of the doctor that his heart was sound he could go for two or three weeks. The emotion of fear, which was created in his mind, was upsetting his heart. It wasn't imaginary. His heart was upset, but only functionally. He was sound structurally.

We say of a person, "He gives me a pain in the neck." He does, because we react in resentment against him. Dr. William Sadler says: "Psychoneurotic pain is not imaginary; it is as real and as distressing to the patient as 'organic' pain, and the accompanying fear and anxiety makes it worse. Since emotional maladjustment is the basis of such fear and anxiety as well as the symptom itself, these reactions are more intense than those based on bonafide organic difficulty."

I once read the account of a man who was studied who had an opening into his stomach. He was observed almost every day for years, and the doctors learned to tell the state of his emotions by the appearance of his stomach lining. Once when the man misplaced some papers, his face grew pale, and the mucose of his stomach grew paler by the minute, as he feared the loss of his job. When the papers were found, his stomach began to regain its normal pink color.

The results of improper emotions are very evident in man's physiological makeup, as well as his social actions. Emotions produce feelings which range from slight tensions to a complete breakdown; from hide to flight. Notice carefully the following summary of the physiological results of emotions.

1. *Cardiac changes* occur after a "startle stimulus." The pulse rate lowers but the heartbeat amplitude increases. There is also a change in the systolic blood pressure.

2. *Respiratory changes* occur when a person becomes highly emotional. A sudden catching of the breath, increased breathing rate, or very irregular breathing may be produced by a sudden change in the emotions.

3. *Glandular secretions* are effected by the emotions. It has been proven that following an emotional stimulation the hydrogen-ion concentration (pH) of saliva is altered. Secretion of adrenalin is increased. In some cases the activity of the sweat glands is greatly increased, as a "cold sweat."

4. *Digestive tract* changes usually follow emotional stimuli. Changes occur in the tonicity of the stomach: sometimes tonus increases and sometimes it decreases. Stomach contractions and intestinal movements are decreased or stopped; salivary and gastric secretions are reduced, and other digestive activities are lessened.

5. *Electrical changes* are produced by emotions as bodily resistance to the passage of a small electric current is decreased. As an index of the emotional status, the psychogalvanic response (P.G.R.) has been widely used.

6. *Brain waves* are changed by emotions. Alpha waves of 8 to 12 cycles per second are shown in non-emotional situations by electroencephalagraph reading. But when emotional topics are introduced, brain waves below 8 cycles per second, delta waves appear.

The whole body reacts to the thoughts in our minds. The young boy who made a speech in Sunday school worked very hard to control his stage fright. Later when asked if he was afraid, he replied, "No, I was not scared, but my stomach was scared."

CONCLUSION

It is not necessary to say that some emotions are all bad and others are all good. For example, fear and anger have a proper place in our lives. They are defensive emotions which prepare us for "flight" or "fight." The challenge, however, is to realize they are less needed in normal living today, especially in their extreme form, than the milder emotions. This is where the need for winning over our emotions comes in, because even a good emotion placed in us through the God-given ability to respond in a certain way may go bad if not controlled.

If you don't win over wrong emotions, those wrong emotions will win over you and your bodily functions. So if you are going to be healthy and happy, you must control your emotions. You cannot let wrong emotions such as fear, anger, resentment, guilt, etc., control your life. The body is "allergic" to them. You are made for love and good deeds, not for fear and hate. Love raises the system, and hate lowers it. Therefore, you must choose your thoughts and emotions wisely. God made you with this capacity; use it; don't abuse it.

In this chapter we have shown that man is an emotional being. The power of emotions is awesome. In a future lesson we will note in detail the role thinking plays in the developing of emotions.

FOR THOUGHT AND DISCUSSION

1. Share an illustration that shows the emotional nature of man.
2. Why do some people play down man's emotions?
3. Why are some emotions healthy?
4. Define emotion.
5. How may negative emotions harm us?
6. Describe how you handle your emotions.
7. How would you help another person get control of his emotions?
8. Why is it harmful for some persons to control their emotions?
9. Which emotions are good? Discuss.
10. What are the major goals of man's emotions?
11. Why are emotions so powerful?
12. Why should we learn how to control our emotions?
13. How do you plan to use this lesson?
14. What additional questions do you have?
15. Suggest some book to read on this subject.

CHAPTER TWO

THE BIBLE AND EMOTIONS

"Thou knowest my downsitting and my uprising, thou understandest my thought afar off" (Psalm 139:2).

INTRODUCTION

One of the most emotional scenes in the Old Testament is the account of Joseph's response when he saw his brother, Benjamin: "And Joseph made haste; for his bowels did yearn upon his brother: and he sought where to weep; and he entered into his chamber, and wept there. And he washed his face, and went out, and refrained himself . . ." (Genesis 43:30, 31).

The Bible provides us with all things that pertain to life and godliness (cf. II Peter 1:3). Throughout its pages we have accounts of people and their emotions. Some of these emotional examples are good, as in the case of Joseph, and some are accounts of how persons violated God's law because they weren't in control of their emotions.

In our last lesson we focused upon man as an emotional being. In this lesson we will study some of his emotions as recorded in the Bible.

BIBLICAL EXAMPLES OF HARMFUL EMOTIONS

A careful study of the following Biblical accounts reveal the consequences of negative emotions which became sinful, or harmful, etc.:

1. *Anger*: Cain killed his brother because of uncontrolled anger in his heart (Genesis 4:1-8).

2. *Fear*: Abraham lied to Abimelech about Sarah because he was afraid of losing his life (Genesis 20:2, 3, 11, 12). Moses ran because of fear (Exodus 2:11-15).

3. *Jealousy and Envy*: Ahab caused the death of Naboth because he was jealous and envious of Naboth's vineyard (I Kings 21:1-14).

4. *Agitation*: King Belshazzar couldn't control his knees from shaking when he saw part of the hand that wrote (Daniel 5:6-9).

5. *Terror*: Eliphaz entered a period of fear and trembling because of a vision he had (Job 4:13-16).

6. *Lust*: David let the emotion of lust lead him into sin (II Samuel 11:1-5; cf. James 1:13-17).

7. *Lust and hatred*: Amnon had strong sexual desires for his sister which led him to rape her, and later hate her (cf. II Samuel 13:2-20).

8. *Greed and covetousness*: Achan brought defeat upon Israel because of his greed and deception (Joshua 7:16-21).

9. *Depression*: King Saul became very depressed when he received God's message from Samuel (I Samuel 28:15-25).

10. *Guilt*: Judas killed himself because of the guilt he felt after betraying Christ (Matthew 27:3-10).

11. *Resentment and hatred*: Saul (apostle Paul) persecuted the church because he resented and hated it (cf. Acts 9:4-9; 26:9-12; Galatians 1:13).

12. *Fear*: Peter denied the Lord because of fear (John 18:15-18).

13. *Pride and arrogance*: Diotrephes was a trouble maker in the early church because of these emotions.

14. *Selfishness*: Ananias and Sapphira lied to God because of the selfishness in their hearts (Acts 5:1-11).

15. *Sorrow*: The rich young ruler, because of sorrow, turned and walked away from an opportunity to follow Jesus (Mark 10:22).

THE EMOTIONS OF GOD

In our study of what the Bible has to say about emotions, we must not overlook the many emotions God ascribes to Himself. While God is spirit (John 4:24), it does not exclude the idea of life, personality and emotions. The Scriptures use many anthropomorphic phrases and words in describing the personality of God. In simple words, God uses language we can understand to teach us that He is not an unfeeling being. Notice the following emotions of God:

1. The *heart* of God is mentioned in Genesis 6:6: "And it repented the Lord that he made man on the earth, and it grieved him at his heart."

2. The rebellion of Israel in the wilderness *grieved* the Lord (Psalm 78:40).

3. God is said to "speak unto them in his *wrath*, and vex them in his sore *displeasure*" (Psalm 2:5).

4. God is pictured as *laughing* at His enemies (Psalm 2:4).

5. The *anger* of Jehovah is mentioned by the prophet Jeremiah (Jeremiah 7:18, 19).

6. The *joy* of God is referred to by the prophet Isaiah (Isaiah 62:5).

7. Everyone knows about the *love* of God as mentioned in John 3:16.

8. The Creator brings *vengeance* upon evil doers (Deuteronomy 32:35).

9. God *hates* graven images that are set up to represent Him or take His place (Deuteronomy 16:21, 22).

10. In Isaiah 53:10 God is referred to as having the ability to experience *pleasure.*

THE EMOTIONS OF CHRIST

The Bible makes it very clear that Jesus took upon himself the nature of a servant (i.e., man in the flesh; Philippians 2:5-8). This is why, therefore, He understands our emotions (cf. Hebrews 4:14, 15). In His case, however, Christ never let His emotions carry Him into sin or wrong doing. He is the perfect example of how good and controlled emotions benefit our lives. He was emotional on many occasions, but they were always appropriate and under control. The point is this: it's okay to be emotional if we handle it like the Lord did.

Take time to study each of the following references. They will impress you with the humanity of Christ: a man of deep feelings and emotions.

1. Jesus was a man of *compassion* (Matthew 9:36). The Greek word *splanchnizomai* refers to being moved inwardly; feelings, emotions.

2. The Son of God experienced proper, controlled *anger* (cf. Mark 3:5). The word for anger is *orge* and suggests a settled condition of mind, even though a strong emotion may be in one's bosom. *Thumos*, the Greek word translated wrath, indicates a more agitated condition of the feelings, an outburst of wrath from inward indignation.

This is not what Christ had. He had *orge*. He was in control of His emotions and actions.

3. Christ *wept* over Lazarus (John 11:35). The Greek word translated wept is *dakruo* and means to shed tears, and is only used in the New Testament of Christ. In Luke 19:41 it is recorded that Christ "wept over Jerusalem." The word here is *klaio* and refers not only to crying but also every outward expression of grief, bewail, mourn for, etc.

4. Prior to the cross He felt *agony* (Luke 22:44). This denotes an inward emotional contest which also touches the conduct of the body. Jesus was in a deep struggle at this time in His life.

5. Jesus *loved* (John 20:2). The love mentioned here is *Phileo* and refers to tender affection.

6. The Master *groaned* in His spirit (John 11:38). The Greek word *embrimaomai* means to be greatly perturbed in mind, deeply moved.

7. Christ *sighed* deeply in His spirit (Mark 8:12; 7:34). *Anastenazo*, the Greek word, suggests a very deeply drawn sigh or groan from within because of feelings.

8. The Lord *cried* out on the cross (Matthew 27:46). It is said that Jesus experienced every form of pain in His death on the cross. Crying was one of the ways He found relief from His pain.

9. Jesus was *sorrowful* and *heavy* in spirit (Matthew 26:37, 38). Again, we see the deep emotions of the Savior while on earth.

10. Christ was a man of *joy* (John 15:11; 17:13). If we are not careful we will think of Jesus only as a suffering Savior and fail to remember such emotions as joy.

11. The Son of God while on earth experienced *loneliness* (cf. Matthew 26:40-46; John 6:15; Luke 9:18). This wasn't because of an inner security weakness, but, rather, because of the agony He felt prior to His death on the cross. He needed the support of the disciples.

12. Christ was able to maintain control of His emotions even as He died on the cross: "Who, when he was reviled, reviled not again; when he suffered, he threatened not; but committed himself to him that judgeth righteously" (I Peter 2:23).

Jesus was not a Stoic who kept Himself above feelings. "Surely he hath borne our griefs, and carried our sorrows: yet we esteem him stricken, smitten of God, and afflicted" (Isaiah 53:4). Thus, as the song says: "Jesus knows all about my troubles." Also, I learn from Him that it is okay to be emotional. The challenge, however, is to keep them within healthy bounds.

THE EMOTIONS OF PAUL

The New Testament Epistles give us a great amount of insight into the emotional life of Paul. Paul's emotions covered the spectrum: from hate to love; from no compassion to compassion; from misguided zeal to controlled zeal, etc. From the day he met Christ, his life was never the same again. Time after time in his writings he reveals his tender, emotional feelings. He was a man of great self-control.

1. Paul had *deep emotional feelings* (i.e., inward affection, bowels) for his brethren (Philippians 1:7, 8; II Corinthians 7:15; Colossians 3:12).

2. Paul *suffered* for Christ (Philippians 1:13, 29, 30). He considered this a blessing.

3. Paul was a man of *joy* (Philippians 2:2, 17). His joy was never determined by his outward circumstances.

4. The great apostle had a *humble* spirit (Philippians 3:4-10; II Corinthians 12:21). He was not puffed up by his own importance.

5. He was a man who had learned to be *content* in every situation (Philippians 4:11). This was a great contributor to his peace of mind. He knew things are the way they are without because things are the way they are within.

6. Paul was a *calm* man even in the face of persecution (Acts 20:24).

7. He had the right attitude toward his "thorn in the flesh" (II Corinthians 12:7-11).

8. Paul did not complain because of his abuses and trials (II Corinthians 11:16-33).

9. Paul was in *travail* for the Galatian brethren (Galatians 4:19).

10. He had great *heaviness* and continual *sorrow* in his heart for the Jews (Romans 9:2).

Again, we see that the Bible presents man as an emotional being. When you become a Christian you are not required to give up your emotions. You are only asked to keep them under control; especially, those that can lead to sin.

IT'S OKAY TO BE EMOTIONAL

In our quest to win over our emotions it should be remembered that God is not asking us to become Stoics, or abandon our ability to feel. If anything, Christianity puts real life and care into our feelings. An old Negro spiritual describes the emotional challenges we face:

"Nobody knows the trouble I've seen;
Nobody knows but Jesus.
Sometimes I'm up, sometimes I'm down–
Oh, yes, Lord!
Sometimes I'm almost to the ground.
Oh, yes, Lord!"

Ups and downs are simply part of life. Medical research has proven that everyone goes through emotional changes during the day. Twenty-five workmen in a railroad shop were checked four times a day to determine their emotional stability, physical condition, and state of mind. Dr. Rexford B. Hersey, of the University of Pennsylvania, found that their charts fell into a fairly regular pattern. There were evenly spaced high and low periods in each man's life. It is these normal emotions that we see in the life of Christ. They are inescapable. Also, they are beneficial to us. It is not possible for a person to always be "high" emotionally; likewise, it is not desireable for him to always be on an emotional "low." God wants us to be in control of the emotions that can harm us physically and spiritually. Whether we are high, low or somewhere in between, we must not permit our emotions to lead us into sin, or into a negative state that will be detrimental to our health.

CONCLUSION

In this lesson we have learned that the Bible is full of examples of man as an emotional being. We have also learned that man's emotions have gotten him into trouble when he hasn't kept them under control.

Jesus is our perfect example of healthy emotions. By studying His life we learn that it is okay to be emotional. It is manly to cry. It is important to permit your emotions to express themselves. He left us an example that we should follow.

The apostle Paul was a man of many emotions. We learn from him that a person can change his emotions if he wants to. Christ gives us power to do so as we yield our lives to Him.

You should be encouraged by the fact that the Bible says it's okay to be emotional. Likewise, you should be challenged by the fact that the Bible motivates us to control our emotions and sin not. This is what winning over emotions is all about!

FOR THOUGHT AND DISCUSSION

1. Discuss Psalm 139:2.
2. Can you think of an additional emotional scene in the Bible? Share it.
3. Why does the Bible reveal harmful emotions?
4. In what sense does God have emotions?
5. List some additional emotions of God and discuss.
6. Why was Jesus emotional?
7. What is your favorite emotion of Christ?
8. Discuss some of Paul's emotions.
9. Can you think of additional emotions Paul exemplified?
10. Why is it okay to be emotional?
11. Why do we go through emotional changes?
12. How does the Biblical teaching about emotions help us?
13. How do you plan to apply this lesson to your life?
14. Do you have additional comments or points to share?
15. How are you coming on your emotional control?

CHAPTER THREE

THE MIND AND EMOTIONS

"As a man thinketh in his heart, so is he" (Proverbs 23:7).

INTRODUCTION

Through her tears and sobs she continually asked: "Why do I feel so much resentment toward Harold everytime he comes into the house?" This frustrated wife and mother was honestly trying to find the answer to this question. Her life and marriage were being destroyed because of the powerful emotion of resentment. Through several counseling sessions she was able to discover what was triggering her emotions. They were being produced by the thoughts within her mind. This awareness became the key for helping her win over resentment.

The other day I was driving down the freeway at 55 miles per hour. Suddenly I saw flashing red and yellow lights in my rear-view mirror. I thought: "What have I done?" as my heart leaped into my throat. As I started to pull over, the police car pulled around me and kept going. Then I thought: "That's great! He is not after me." My emotions were back to normal in a matter of seconds. What caused this emotional surge? I *thought* I was going to be stopped and given a ticket. My emotions responded to my thought. I had placed a wrong interpretation on one fact: The police car was coming up behind me with its lights blinking, and I didn't think of other reasons why it was happening. Thus my distorted view and interpretation of the fact produced my emotion. My emotions responded to the signal my mind sent them. This is a vital truth in our quest to win over our emotions. It is not the actual event but your perception that result in changes in your moods.

You determine your emotions by the choice of thoughts you hold and believe. Emotions are not external entities which enter into our bodies arbitrarily like a germ. Your emotions, regardless of their nature, are the product of your thoughts. Therefore, correct thinking is essential to winning over your emotions. This also means that emotions are not controlled by external forces (or actions of others). You are in the driver's seat. You select your emotions when you select your thoughts. You feel the way you do right now because of the thoughts you are presently thinking. Change your thinking and you will change your emotions.

There are many things which influence the way we think. The five senses are the doors to the mind, especially the ears and eyes. This is why, therefore, we must be very careful about what we permit to enter into our minds through our ears or eyes. Paul put it this way: "Be not deceived; God is not mocked: for whatsoever a man soweth, that shall he also reap" (Galatians 6:8). Sowing negative thoughts produce negative emotions.

It was Mary's first day on the job. She had studied long and hard to prepare herself for the secretarial position she now had. As she was being introduced to the other ladies in the office, her heart began to beat faster and her palms became sweaty. "Of all times," she thought, "to get a case of nerves, now is not the time." The more she thought about it the worse she became. Mary was suffering from a case of "new job" anxiety. Her emotions were causing her great discomfort. Later she was able to realize that her emotional problem was produced by thinking, as she was meeting the other women, "I bet they are all better typists than I am." This triggered her emotions.

THINK RIGHT TO FEEL RIGHT

How do you feel? The answer to this question depends on what you are thinking at this moment. If you are thinking positive thoughts your response may be, "I feel great!" On the other hand if your frame of mind is negative you may say, "I don't feel so hot," or "I feel lousy."

As human beings we create our moods by the thoughts we think. A thought comes into your mind and if you believe it, you will experience an immediate emotional response. A housewife may start to think that the meal she has prepared for her husband's boss is going to be a big failure. In a few minutes she is feeling depressed and a headache makes things worse. Your thoughts, unless you have an organic disorder, create emotions which bring on depression and headaches. It doesn't matter that the housewife has a great reputation for being a good cook, she has let negativity take control of her life. She has lost her "peace of mind" through twisted thinking.

There is no more fundamental truth than, "As a man thinketh in his heart, so is he" (Proverbs 23:7). All of your up and down feelings are produced by your emotional response to thoughts in your mind. You always get emotionally what you think. If you sow a negative thought, you will reap a negative crop of emotions. Conversely, if you sow positive thoughts, you will reap a positive crop of emotions. This is the law of sowing and reaping (cf. Galatians 6:5-8).

Sam, at age 40, was becoming a nervous wreck and a hypochrondriac. He had developed an obsession with his health. He was reading self-diagnosis health books trying to find out if he had the disease he thought he had. Every new pain, bump, pimple, burp, etc., was a "sure sign" that he had the disease. He would break out in a cold sweat and grow weak when he would read about some disease and its symptoms in the newspaper. He just knew he had the disease.

Sam is a classic example of what I call twisted thinking. He would read words and interpret them through a series of negative thoughts which produced internal self-talk. His mind would process the thoughts, not actual facts or events, and produce emotional responses such as fatigue, nervousness, anxiety, depression, loss of appetite, and a host of others. Through twisted thinking, Sam created his problems.

Sam's case has a happy ending. He learned and applied the truth – ***Feelings aren't facts.*** Through learning that his negative thoughts created his negative emotions, and thus they weren't accurate, Sam straightened his twisted thinking. He learned how to react and control his thinking, as well as knowing that he couldn't keep some negative thoughts from popping into his mind, but he had control over what he would do with them. He chose to eject them. Everyone of us must learn the art of mental ejection: the ability to eject defeating thoughts from our mind.

Failure and negative thoughts, which produce twisted thinking, need to be promptly ejected from our mind. Overcoming thoughts need to be warmly welcomed, entertained, and encouraged. Paul wrote, "Let this attitude be in you, which was also in Christ Jesus" (Philippians 2:5). Your attitude is the prevailing force in your life; your attitude is the result of your thinking. If you want to change your life you must change your thinking. Your mind is the seat of all emotions.

Saul of Tarsus is a good Biblical example of twisted thinking. In his defense before Agrippa, he acknowledged the results of his twisted thinking. He said: "I verily thought with myself, that I ought to do many things contrary to the name of Jesus of Nazareth. Which thing I also did in Jerusalem: and many of the saints did I shut up in prison, having received authority from the chief priests; and when they were put to death, I gave my voice against them" (Acts 26:9, 10).

The prime-mover behind Paul's actions and emotions, according to his own confession, was his thinking: "I verily *thought* with myself . . ." He was the product of what he permitted to enter his mind; namely, negative and false teachings about Christ and Christianity. He thought both were wrong and needed to be done away with.

Later, through proper instruction which he accepted, he was able to straighten his twisted thinking.

It has been proven over and over that the body (or emotion) doesn't know the difference between an established fact and an erroneous fact. The thing that matters is how the mind handles what comes into it. I know of an example where a man received a phone call and thought the caller said his father was dying with a heart attack. He jumped into his car and drove as fast as he could to his father's house, only to be greeted by his father at the door. The son almost had a heart attack himself. Why? His emotions were responding to thoughts the mind were holding as true. In his mind he believed his father was dying; thus, his body acted accordingly. Later he learned the caller had said "John," instead of "Don," who was a friend of the family.

KEYS TO WINNING

We need to recognize that our thought patterns and habits can be changed constructively and we can experience release from twisted thinking, reactions and responses that continually defeat us. The following keys will provide a framework for straightening twisted thinking.

1. Recognize YOU are in control of your thoughts. God created you with this wonderful ability.

2. Don't try to suppress your thoughts. Burying them only reinforces the negative response demonstrated in your emotions. We must be alert to these thoughts as they come into our minds and say "NO" to them, and saying "YES" to a positive replacement.

3. When you are challenged by a twisted thought, ask yourself, "Why am I thinking this way? What has 'triggered' this negative thought?" Determining the stimulus is a must.

4. At the very suggestion of a defeating thought, eject it from your mind with a positive Bible verse. Notice the words of Paul, "Fix your thoughts on what is true and good and right. Think about things that are pure and lovely, and dwell on the fine, good things in others. Think about all you can praise God for and be glad about" (Philippians 4:8, *Living Bible*).

5. Changing your thinking takes place as an act of the will. Paul said, "Set your minds on things above" (Colossians 3:2). This declarative statement involves an act of the will. *You set* your mind. "Put to death . . . whatever belongs to your earthly nature: sexual immorality, impurity, lust, evil desires" (verse 5), "*You* must rid yourselves" (verse 8), "Put on" (verse 12, NASB).

6. You can't control what others say about you or think about you, but you can control how you react to it (cf. Proverbs 25:28). Our desire is not to rid ourselves of our emotions, but, rather, learn how to control them with God's help.

7. Pray to God for wisdom and strength. He has promised to give if we pray in faith (cf. James 1:2-5). Through God's word, prayer and a definite plan of action you can win over twisted thinking.

CONCLUSION

We need to face life in the spirit of the man who lost his eyesight. He rushed to the doctor. The treatment by the physician made it possible for him to see again, but the return of his sight caused the loss of his memory. He returned to the doctor. This time he was treated for a loss of memory. The man regained his memory but lost his eyesight again.

"Well," said the physician, "we can't cure both together, so you'll have to choose between sight and memory. Which will it be?"

The man answered, "Eyesight! I'd rather see where I'm going than to know where I've been." This is the positive way to look at life and the past because the next step is much more important than the last step. It doesn't matter that you have been plagued in the past with twisted thinking or warped emotions, the next step you take to handle it is what counts.

FOR THOUGHT AND DISCUSSION

1. Discuss Proverbs 23:7.
2. Have you had an experience like my freeway example? Share it.
3. How do we determine our emotions?
4. List some things that influence how we think.
5. What produces up and down feelings?
6. Define twisted thinking.
7. Give a Bible example of twisted thinking.
8. How can you correct wrong thinking?
9. Do you practice positive thinking?
10. Discuss Philippians 4:8.
11. Discuss Colossians 3:2.
12. How do you plan to use this lesson?
13. Do you have any additional thoughts about this lesson?
14. What would you say to a person who said, "I can't control my thoughts"?
15. Share three ideas for improving your thinking.

CHAPTER FOUR

INNER WINNING AND EMOTIONS

"Things are the way they are without because things are the way they are within."

INTRODUCTION

You will never be a real winner over your emotions until you win the inner battles of life. The control panel for all your emotional control is within your mind. It's under your direction and power. You call the shots.

A group of business men, who were members of a prominent social club, decided on a unique humanitarian project for the group. They appointed two men to go down to the skid row section of the city and find a derelict they could help become a success in life. When they found the right person he was taken to a luxurious room in a hotel rented just for him. After a shower, shave and a good meal, the bum was taken to a barber shop for the works (i.e., haircut, facial, manicure, etc.); from the barber shop he was taken to a tailor's shop and fitted with a wardrobe of expensive clothes.

The men of the club felt a deep sense of satisfaction from helping the man. He looked right at home when he was introduced to the group. In fact, one member of the club gave the once bum a good job with his company. After a week on the job the man failed to report to work. After a couple of days the employer went to the hotel to see what had happened, only to learn that his new employee hadn't stayed in his room or eaten in the hotel restaurant in several days. After additional checking, he found the derelict in a cheap hotel on skid row.

The men of the club were shocked when they heard the report on what had happened to the subject of their project. What had happened to the person who just a few days before looked like a successful business man? What made him go back to his old way of life? Inside the man was STILL THE SAME. A changing of his external appearance and living environment didn't change the inner man. He was still the same "old man" inside, with the same old ways of thinking.

A person will never become a real winner in life merely by making a few external changes. To really win in the game of life a person must be an *inner winner*. Conversely, a person may never be a winner according to the standards of the world, but if he has won the battle over the inner man, he is a real winner. Inner winning is what real, joyful, content living is all about. Inner winning is a position you can maintain regardless of what is happening in your external world. Inner winning doesn't depend on someone being a loser, or a contest; it goes beyond the win-lose philosophy being pursued by the world. Inner victory comes from a positive spiritual attitude; and is not based upon how well you perform or don't perform. Inner winning puts you in charge of your emotions. You push the buttons of your choice.

INNER WINNING IS BIBLICAL

The inner winner principle is sound, workable and exciting because it is based upon God's word. Jesus had this to say about it: "Woe unto you scribes and Pharisees, hypocrites! for ye make clean the outside of the cup and of the platter, but WITHIN they are full of extortion and excess. Thou blind Pharisee, cleanse first that which is WITHIN the cup and platter, that the outside of them may be clean also" (Matthew 23:25, 26). To look on the outward works and appearance of the Pharisees, you would think of them as real winners. They were the epitome of success in religious practices. But Jesus strips them bare and takes us into their hearts. They were losers!

The Master, who knew what was within man, made it

very clear that a person's wrong overt action is the result of not being an inner winner. All sin has its beginning within the mind of man. Jesus said: "For from WITHIN, out of the heart of men, proceed EVIL THOUGHTS, adulteries, fornication, murders, thefts, covetousness, wickedness, deceit, lasciviousness, an evil eye, blasphemy, pride, foolishness: All these evil things come from WITHIN, and defile the man" (Mark 7:21-23). A lack of outward control is a sure sign of poor (or no) inward control.

The inner winner knows that no one person is better than anyone else. He feels good about the fact that we are all created in the image of God (cf. Genesis 1:27-29). He also realizes that God holds us all accountable for only the abilities we have as individuals (cf. Matthew 25:14-30). The Father doesn't judge one son on the basis of his being able to out-do his brother or sister. The only battle he must win is the flesh against the spirit (cf. Galatians 5: 16-26). The major goals of his life are not set by the world or some other person. He is striving to have the attitude of Christ (cf. Philippians 2:5-8), and live faithful unto death (cf. Revelation 2:10). He has *learned* that contentment doesn't depend on what you have of this world's goods, or everything being just right in your environment (cf. Philippians 4:11). The child of God knows that he "can do all things through Christ" (Philippians 4:13).

The inner winner knows the value of right thinking. He accepts as truth that a man is the way he is because of the way he thinks in his heart (cf. Proverbs 23:7). The inner winner has real peace because he has learned HOW to think as well as WHAT to think. Paul's program serves as his guideline: "Finally brethren, whatsoever things are true, whatsoever things are honest, whatsoever things are just, whatsoever things are pure, whatsoever things are lovely, whatsoever things are of a good report; if there be any virtue, and if there be any praise, THINK on these things" (Philippians 4:8). This is real power for emotion control.

Your attitude is one thing that you have complete

control over. It is within your power to make it positive or to make it negative. You can start becoming an inner winner at any time. The choice is yours. In Christianity there are no losers where faith is the guiding principle; and growth into the fulness of Christ is the goal (cf. Ephesians 4:11-16). The only loser is the person who turns away from His Lord (cf. Hebrews 10:24-31). Christ has not called us to be losers but to be "more than conquerors" (Romans 8:37).

To be a real, Biblical winner you must release all that you are toward becoming like Jesus Christ in every situation. Losing, then, would be not releasing your total self toward becoming like Christ in EVERY situation. The inner winner always sees himself as a Christian. His objective is to make a faith response to all of God's promises and commandments.

How does the inner winner face the challenges of life? Let me share with you how one brother did; a brother in Christ whose funeral I conducted last week. At age 52, Don Monday came face-to-face with the reality that he had cancer spread throughout his body, and life for him on this earth wasn't going to last much longer. His interests turned to spiritual matters and the promises of God in the Bible. After several weeks of study, Don obeyed the gospel. During the four months which followed his conversion, he kept a positive attitude toward his disease and toward the Father in heaven. He attended church services in pain; he studied God's word and found the strength to win over the situation. One day as I was visiting him in the hospital, I noticed a hand written note on the wall across from Don's bed. It read: "When faced with death I will not quit," and his name was signed to it. Don didn't quit. Through pain and suffering he continued to trust the Lord. At the time when his physical strength had failed him, Don was able to be an inner winner. His moment of death came after his wife, who was holding him in her arms, finished reading the Twenty-Third Psalm. When she said "Amen"; Don won his last inner victory and went to be with the Lord.

Being an inner winner is not easy. It requires desire and work to make it a reality. But with God's help, and through His word, we can all become more of an inner winner today than we were yesterday, and if we do, THE BEST IS YET TO BE!

WINNING THROUGH SELF-DISCIPLINE

Self-discipline determines which emotional button you will push in every situation of life. Inner winning is possible through self-control.

Do you remember the last time you resolved to make a specific change in your life? Perhaps you vowed to lose weight; stop smoking; stop procrastinating; become a better parent; grow in knowledge; quit worrying; etc. In your mind you determined to change. "This time," you told yourself, "I mean it; I am going to accomplish my goal; I am going to become the person God wants me to be!" In a few days or weeks, however, the resolve had lost its fire and you were back in the same old rut. You have read self-help articles and books and decided, "From now on I . . ." but today you are basically like you have always been, there hasn't been much change. You mean well, but nothing seems to *work* for you; you have tried, but always seem to come up short of your goal.

Here you are again, reading a book on self-discipline. If you are not careful this will be just another self-help lesson that you will soon forget. As you began this section you may have thought, "Another lesson on an impossible subject; full of impractical platitudes; I'll read it anyway." Let me encourage you to continue reading with an open and determined mind, because one of the major keys to your successes in life is SELF-DISCIPLINE.

Bob Considine, in his book *They Rose Above It*, tells one of the most remarkable stories about self-discipline I have ever read. The story centers around the father of one of ninety-five children burned to death in the fire that destroyed Chicago's Lady of the Angels school in December 1958. Considine graphically relates the account of the father as he approaches the open grave where his son will be buried:

> *"He had little or no visible face of human skin. He wore a startling leather mask that reached down from his hairline to his sensitive mouth. Out of the right side of the horrid covering, at eye level, protruded what appeared to be a jeweler's eyepiece with a pinpoint opening instead of a full lens. He stood there, erect and silent on the arm of a male member of the mourning party . . . 'He just came from the hospital against the doctor's wishes. He had an operation for a detached retinas a few days ago. They told him that if he cries at the funeral the salt of his tears will enter the incisions and destroy his sight forever'." (Page 44)*

The father left the funeral without crying. Even though his heart was breaking his eyes held back the tears. What discipline! What a story! Especially in a day of cowardice and little self-discipline. Men can control themselves when they have to, or really want to through self-discipline. This is inner winning!

Successful living and emotional control occurs through self-control, and self-control comes through self-discipline. The Proverb writer said, "He that hath no rule over his own spirit is like a city that is broken down, and without walls" (Proverbs 25:28). Dr. Maxwell Maltz, in his book *Creative Living For Today*, says, "Self-discipline is your golden key, without it you cannot be happy. Discipline is the difference between what we *can* do and what we *should* do. In our creative day, we live with discipline continuing to set goals, refusing to permit termites of nothingness to empty us as human beings." Self-discipline is a power source for inner winning.

To the ears of many in our day discipline is a dirty

word. It is an affront to many children when they are told to do their homework, pick up their room, take out the garbage, etc. They have developed, in many cases, their lack of discipline from undisciplined parents who indulge themselves without restraint. Have you ever noticed how many times overweight parents have overweight children? Parents are powerful models for developing self-discipline in the home. They must teach as well as demonstrate self-control in order to train their children in this great virtue. Inner winners can help others win over the trials of life.

Self-discipline is a Bible doctrine and is essential to Christian growth. Peter wrote: "And beside this, giving all diligence, add to your faith virtue; and to virtue knowledge; and to knowledge self-control; and to self-control patience . . ." (II Peter 1:5, 6). The Greek word for self-control is *egkrateia* and refers to the "holding of passions and desires in hand." The word was used of one who masters his desires and passions, especially his sensual appetites. In Titus 1:8 the word is used in reference to an elder "holding himself in control." In Galatians 5:23 it is listed as a fruit of the Spirit. Self-control was part of the message Paul shared with Felix (Acts 24:25). The Christian, therefore, must be in control of himself. There are no shortcuts to winning over our emotions.

KEYS TO SELF-DISCIPLINE

You and I both know that self-discipline is not an easy thing to accomplish. It is a continual daily effort. When Paul told Timothy that he must discipline himself for the purpose of godliness (I Timothy 4:7), he used a word (*gumnazo*) which related to athletics. An athelete becomes an expert only by years of hard work and practice. Hank Aaron didn't become the homerun king just by being on a ball team and coming to bat several times during each game. He worked hard on his batting skills, spending hours on the practice field. This is what a

Christian must do if he ever hopes to master his life. In conjunction with daily practice the following keys will also help in developing self-discipline.

1. It all begins in your mind. The attitude you hold toward self-discipline will determine your success (Proverbs 23:7). You must believe you can control yourself. There are no shortcuts to winning over your emotions.

2. Don't be afraid to pinpoint your weak areas. Do a complete self-examination on yourself. Do you have a temper? Do you eat too much? Do you gossip? Do you worry?

3. Try to determine why you lack proper self-discipline. What Bible verses are you violating? Have you really tried to win over the problem area?

4. Tackle your weakness without reservation. Confront it with a specific plan of action. Don't be afraid to ask others to help you.

5. Start your discipline program in small areas. Get out of bed promptly. Write that letter. Pay that bill on time. Hang up your clothes. Arrive on time. Have the meal on time, etc. Little successes lead to bigger victories later. Visualize the result of being in control of yourself. Relax, close your eyes and see yourself twenty pounds lighter. Imagine how you will feel as a slimmer person.

6. Fill your mind with positive challenges and directives from God's word. The Psalmist said, "O how love I thy law! it is my meditation all the day" (Psalm 119:97).

7. Learn to roll with the punches. There will be days when things don't go the way you planned. Worrying and fretting is foolish. Take each set back as one of the "all things" that work for your good (cf. Romans 8:28).

8. Don't forget it is a daily challenge which centers in "self-denial" as taught by Christ (cf. Matthew 16:24), as well as daily cross bearing and following Him. Examine your commitment each day. Have I denied myself today?

9. Pray for wisdom on a daily basis. God will answer your prayer (cf. James 1:5).

10. Don't quit because you have a few failures. Hank Aaron struck out many times, but he didn't quit. A person who is trying to lose weight may conclude after eating a piece of forbidden pie that he might as well give up dieting. This is wrong thinking. Don't quit!

11. Don't be afraid to be hard on yourself. Paul knew that he must "buffet" his body if he expected to win the self-control battle. We must endure hardship as a good soldier of Christ.

12. Don't forget your goal is to develop a new *habit*. When you do something long enough it becomes part of you. You can practice a positive habit just as easy as an old one (or wrong one). The key is *practice*.

CONCLUSION

Self-discipline is an exciting challenge that the Lord will help you accomplish in your life. It is a must for inner winning and emotional control. The key is to make the commitment and then follow through on it with *daily action*. If you will do this, you will become a more self-disciplined person, and THE BEST IS YET TO BE!

FOR THOUGHT AND DISCUSSION

1. Define inner winning.
2. Why don't external changes produce inner changes?

3. How does Matthew 23:25, 26 apply to this subject?

4. How is a person defiled?

5. When can you start becoming an inner winner?

6. What is the biggest obstacle to inner winning?

7. "________________ determines which emotional button you will push in every situation of life."

8. Why is it difficult to keep resolutions?

9. Define self-discipline.

10. Do you know a good example of self-discipline? Share it.

11. Discuss Proverbs 25:28.

12. Do you have a personal plan for self-discipline?

13. How do you plan to use this material?

14. What additional questions do you have?

15. Give a Bible example of self-control.

CHAPTER FIVE

IMAGINATION AND EMOTIONS

"The soul without imagination is what an observatory would be without a telescope." H. W. Beecher

INTRODUCTION

Grandmother saw Johnny running around the house straddling a stick and slapping himself and asked why.

"Well," said Johnny, "I just got tired of walking and thought I'd ride my horse for a while."

All of us remember illustrations like this from our own childhood. With very few toys, we kept ourselves entertained through the creative use of our imaginations. One hour we would be cowboys, then the next hour we would be indians.

The role of imagination in daily living is powerful. It plays a major part in helping us maintain sound mental health. God created us with the ability to imagine. Almost every action is preceded by a mental picture. William Blake said, "What is now proven was once only imagined." George Eliot wrote, "We are all of us imaginative in some form or other, for images are the brood of desire." Thus, as Napoleon said, "Imagination rules the world." And I might add—especially the inner world of man's being.

Proper use of imagination is one of the most important keys to winning over your emotions.

POWER OF IMAGINATION

I don't know if you have thought about it or not, but most, if not all, of our thinking occurs in mental pictures. For example when you hear the word, river, a picture comes into your mind of a stream of water. Try to think of some exception to this basic rule. Some persons are referred to as having photographic minds. What this is really saying is that a certain person does a better job in using his mind than most of us do. In a very real sense all of us have photographic minds. The challenge is to use this God-given ability with greater proficiency.

After God created man, He pronounced that he was good. This pronouncement included man's imagination. Later, however, because of sin, God said about man: " . . . God saw that the wickedness of man was great in the earth, and that every imagination of the thoughts of his heart was only evil continually" (Genesis 6:5).

What does imagination have to do with emotions? Everything! Napoleon Hill wrote: "The imagination is literally the workshop wherein are fashioned all plans created by man. The impulse, the desire is given shape, form, and action through the aid of the imaginative faculty of the mind."

In 1943, in a London bomb shelter after a severe air raid, 200 people were found dead. There were no bomb injuries. All had died from fright. One can easily begin to think how these people must have let their imaginations run wild with them.

Dr. Maxwell Maltz wrote: "Imagination plays a far more important role in our lives than most of us realize . . . we act, or fail to act, not because of 'will', as is so commonly believed, but because of imagination . . . Your nervous system reacts appropriately to what 'you' *think* or imagine to be true . . . It follows that if our ideas and mental images concerning ourselves are distorted or unrealistic, then our reaction to our environment will likewise be inappropriate."

I once heard a story about a lady who was obsessed with the belief that she had a frog in her stomach. In fear and frustration, she went to see a doctor. After a physical examination, the physician tried to convince her that it was not possible for a frog to live in her stomach. "Are you calling me a liar? I feel the frog. I feel him jumping up and down inside of me!"

The lady went to one doctor after another, always with the same results. Finally she met a very understanding physician. He said, "I believe you, madam. Why don't you come to the hospital tomorrow morning? We shall remove the frog."

The doctor used practical psychology. He gave her anesthesia, but didn't operate. He went downtown and bought a frog, put it in a jar, and came back to the bedside of the lady. "Here is your frog" he said. "How do you feel now?" She jumped right off of her bed, hugged the doctor and stated that she felt wonderful and was now well.

At home, she placed the jar which contained the frog on the mantle and invited her friends to see it, as proof to them that she had been right after all, and that it wasn't all in her imagination. She felt wonderful until one of her friends remarked, "Gee, I hope the frog hasn't laid any eggs!"

It is not hard to imagine what happened to this lady. The power of the imagination is awesome. Many of our emotional problems and hangups come from the negative input we give our minds. There is a lot of truth in this statement: *What you see is what you get.*

The power of imagination may be used for good or bad. Bernard Haldane wrote: "For example, imagination certainly could be important to your success. Without it you would not be able to imagine yourself being more successful than you are now, and so would have no incentive to move." Daniel C. Stone wrote: "Only your imagination limits you as you grow."

Dr. Irving Oyle, in his book *The Healing Mind* has this to say about the affect imagination has on emotions: "I might decide, for example, that I always hated the sight of Grandma. In that case the sight of her image upon my visual cortex would precipitate the appropriate emotion—anger. Conversely, I could selectively recall only pleasant memories, thus deciding that the sight of my dear departed Grandma's . . . image fills me with joy, or grief, perhaps even pain" (p. 86). Dr. Oyle believes that "we create specific emotions by our mental decisions" (*ibid*, p. 86).

Dr. O. Carl Simonton, at the world-famous Cancer Counseling and Research Center in Fort Worth, Texas, has documented the amazing role of imagination in fighting cancer. "Relaxation and mental imagery are among the most valuable tools we have found to help patients learn to believe in their ability to recover from cancer. In fact, we mark as the conception of our present approach the first time Carl used mental imagery with a patient. Since then, we have discovered that mental imagery is not only an effective motivational tool for recovering health, but is also an important tool for self-discovery and for making creative change in other areas of life."

There have been many amazing stories come to us from the Vietnam War. There is an interesting one about a pilot who was in solitary confinement. He fought within himself to retain his sanity. To do this, he mentally pictured his release, freedom, boarding the plane home, the flight, and his reunion with his family. He went through these steps thousands of times. They became real to him. The daily use of his imagination saved his life. He was able to endure, and was finally released.

Your imagination is a powerful tool for emotional control. This is why you must learn to properly use it.

DEFINING IMAGINATION

Some readers of this book may be surprised that it contains a chapter on imagination. This is true because of the wrong concepts people have about imagination; others are ignorant as to its role in our daily living. Some think it is a non-Biblical subject; others think it belongs in the field of psychic science; and a few believe it is an exercise in daydreaming, etc. These attitudes exist in spite of the fact that *every person* has an imagination and uses it moment by moment. Just because there have been some errors taught about the use and place of imagination, doesn't mean that there isn't a valid, useable body of truth about the subject. Imagination is as vital to life as breathing; without it man would be no more than an animal.

Before I share some specific definitions of imagination, I will state *some things that positive imagination is not.*

First, it is not an exercise in fantasizing. Most fantasies are not based upon facts. The list of fantasies that people indulge in are endless. Sex and financial success are two of the major ones. The media exploits it to the fullest. Disillusionment is the end result of most fantasies.

Second, it is not a dream-world existence. An extreme case of this is the man who thought he was Napoleon. Concerning this practice, one writer said, "It is the fine art of making a fool out of yourself."

Third, it is not a substitute for reality. Christians, above all people, are supposed to face the realities of life. Our hope of victory is placed in God's power (cf. Ephesians 3:20). It is a reality that man has an imagination that can be used for good.

Fourth, it is not hypnosis. Some people have a deep fear of being hypnotized. Others believe hypnosis is of the devil. The use of your ability to imagine has nothing to do with hypnosis. God expects each of us to do our own thinking (cf. Proverbs 23:7).

Fifth, it is not escapism. Many persons try to use their imaginations to escape from the burdens of life. Truth is the only valid and beneficial reality of life. Jesus said, "Ye shall know the truth and the truth shall set you free" (John 8:32).

Sixth, it is not a method to induce sin. A person can sin through the wrong use of his imagination. Jesus said,

"Whosoever looketh on a woman to lust after her hath committed adultery with her already in his heart" (Matthew 5:28). Many psychologists and sociologists praise such evil use of the imagination, but God condemns it (cf. Romans 1:20-28).

Seventh, it is not a parlor game. There is nothing wrong with using the imagination in games. The challenge, however, is not to live in a world of continual foolishness and play.

Eighth, it is not a higher conscience experience. Some people teach that through metaphysical speculations of the mind, we will become better persons, and have power over all life's problems. This is wrong thinking, and using the imagination in a way God hasn't intended.

Ninth, it is not Transcendental Meditation. TM, as it is popularly referred to, makes such claims as: projecting your mind into others; supernatural power of ESP; mystic powers; astral projection, etc. These are anti-Biblical teachings and must be rejected by Christians. Using your imagination has nothing to do with the false teachings of TM.

Tenth, it is not pretending. This is just another way of day-dreaming or trying to escape from reality. There are real problems that exist in our lives, which a creative and proper use of the imagination can help us handle.

I think because of the discussion so far you have a good grasp on how I am using the word imagination. It would be well, however, to take a moment at this point in our study to give a clear, workable definition of imagination.

Webster defines it as: "the act or power of forming mental images of what is not actually present . . . anything imagined; mental image; creation in mind."

Unger, in his *Bible Dictionary*, defines it as: " . . . the image-making, pictorial faculty of the mind, reproducing and recombing former thoughts and experiences."

Imagination, therefore, is a function created within man by God to perceive (or picture) that which is not present to the senses. It is the ability of the mind's eye to "see". It is the ability to "feel". The soul has "ears". The builder "sees" the house even before he drives the first stake. Columbus "saw" America even before he sailed from Europe. Beethoven "heard" music in his mind even though he was nearly deaf. The lady was sick because she "felt" the frog jumping.

Everybody has an imagination that is creative in one way or another. Imagination is a fact of life. You can't escape from it no matter how hard you try. The challenge, therefore, is to bring it under control through God's power. It will give you peace of mind or it will make life wretched.

The most important product of a person's imagination is the self-image he holds of himself. How you "see" yourself will usually determine how you will act. A lot of man's emotional problems come from his inferiority complexes. Through changing one's self-image, he changes his life. It occurs in the powerful imagination.

THE BIBLE AND IMAGINATION

Since God created man with the ability to imagine, and since it is a fact that his imagination can lead him into sin, we shouldn't be surprised, therefore, to learn that the Bible has a great deal to say about it. Study carefully the following verses.

1. Man can *commit evil* through the wrong use of his imagination (cf. Genesis 6:5; 8:21; Deuteronomy 31:21).

2. There are many *good things* that should be kept in the imagination (cf. I Chronicles 29:18).

3. *Wrong doing* comes from the imagination of the mind (cf. Deuteronomy 29:19).

4. *God knows* our imagination (Deuteronomy 31:21).

5. Man *walks* according to what he imagines in his heart (cf. Jeremiah 13:10; 16:12).

6. The *thoughts produce* our imaginations (Proverbs 6:18).

7. Man's *reasoning* involves his imagination (cf. Romans 1:21; II Corinthians 10:5).

8. *Understanding* involves the imagination (cf. Luke 1:51).

9. Each person is *responsible* for the imagery he holds in mind (cf. Ezekiel 8:12).

10. God *does not want* us to use our imagination for evil (Zechariah 8:17; Psalm 140:2).

11. *Perfect peace* is promised to those who have their minds (i.e., imagination, Hebrew, *yetser*) set on God (cf. Isaiah 26:3).

12. We must be *spiritually minded* (cf. Romans 8:6). This is the greatest use of the imagination (cf. Philippians 2:5).

Therefore, since the imagination is a Bible subject, we should be excited about studying it (cf. II Timothy 2:15).

HOW TO USE IMAGINATION TO WIN

It is a proven fact that you act, and feel, not according to the way things are, but according to the picture your mind holds of what they are like. We act, feel and behave the way we do because of the result of our mental images.

Therefore, in order to win over a negative or undesirable emotion, you must use your positive imagination. You must "see" yourself winning over emotions.

Through imagination (i.e., visualization) you can confront and win your emotional wars. You can use your God-given mind to picture the harmful emotion you are dealing with. In your mind you can "practice" new attitudes, conduct, feelings, situations and positive conduct, which at this point you may be refraining from doing. Through mental performing, you will have the same impact on your nervous system as actually performing the real thing. In time positive picturing will become positive conduct. The following guidelines will help you use your imagination to win over emotional challenges.

First, you must find a place where you can be alone and relax. There are many approaches to relaxing. I will leave it up to you to find the one that suits your needs. Also, set aside at least 30 minutes for this relaxation period.

Second, in your mind visualize a large screen upon which to display your mind-pictures. Practice until this becomes easy. For example in your relaxed state try to see an orange on your mental screen; a car; a friend's face, etc.

Third, picture the situation (or thing) that you want to win over. This will be hard because it is uncomfortable. If you resent or hate a person, see yourself acting positive toward him/her.

Fourth, remove the old harmful pictures from your mind. If you continue to view mind pictures of yourself as fear haunted and defeated, you will allow these false pictures to hinder the development of positive ones.

Fifth, hold the positive picture for several minutes. Dr. Harry Emerson Fosdick wrote: "Hold a picture of yourself long and steadily enough in your mind's eye and you will be drawn toward it. Picture yourself vividly as defeated and that alone will make victory impossible. Picture yourself vividly as winning and that alone will contribute immeasureably to success. Great living starts with a picture, held in your imagination, of what you would like to do or be."

Sixth, practice your visualization until you get the victory. Habits of weeks, months or years don't just go away after one session of visualization. It takes time and patience.

Seventh, concentrate during your sessions. Your mind will want to dart here and there during your visualization periods. Keep it on the screen of your mind. You are the director of the movies you show on your mental screen.

Mary, at age 25, had a terrible fear of riding elevators. Upon suggestion from a counselor, and after some teaching, she spent 30 minutes each day in a relaxed position, picturing herself going through the process of riding an elevator. After six weeks she was able, with help from her husband, to ride an elevator. She was still afraid, but she was now in control of her fear.

George, a deacon in the church, was wrestling with a strong case of resentment against a preacher. On certain days it moved him into the anger zone. He was miserable and unhappy because of these emotions. After hearing a lecture on the role of imagination in winning over emotions, he decided to put the guidelines into practice. He pictured himself being loving, forgiving and friendly toward the preacher. In a matter of weeks he found his feelings and actions changing. He was practicing what he had been visualizing.

CONCLUSION

Not only must we be aware of the role that imagination plays in forming our emotions, we must also realize the positive role it has in winning over undesirable ones. This is what I have stressed in this lesson.

In the remainder of this book we will discuss various emotions, that if not properly controlled, will cause unhappiness, frustration, etc. You will be constantly reminded of the role of imagination in winning your daily victories. Thus, let me encourage you to master the material in this chapter because you will be using it from now on. As you use your creative imagination, THE BEST IS YET TO BE!

FOR THOUGHT AND DISCUSSION

1. How important is imagination to life?
2. Define imagination.
3. How does Genesis 6:5 relate to this lesson?
4. Discuss: "What you see is what you get" in relation to imagination.
5. What role does imagination play in disease cure?
6. Why is imagination misunderstood?
7. Discuss some of the things imagination is not.
8. Why are some person's imaginations better than others?
9. Discuss the points relating to the Bible and imagination.
10. Have you ever practiced visualization? Share.
11. Do you personally use visualization for emotional control? Have you ever?
12. How do you plan to use this lesson?
13. What additional points do you have?
14. Have you read a good book on visualization? Discuss.
15. What is creative imagination?

CHAPTER SIX

EMOTIONS AND PHYSICAL EXERCISE

"For physical training is of some value . . ." (I Tim. 4:8, NIV).

INTRODUCTION

There is an old tale about a monastery in Portugal that was built on the top of a 350 foot cliff. To get to the top and visit the monastery visitors were pulled up in a wicker basket by an old rope. On one occasion a visitor stepped into the basket for the descent, and asked, "How often do you get a new rope?"

"Whenever the old one breaks," replied a monk calmly.

In our rushing, changing, I-don't-have-time-world, many are traveling down the highway of life with little concern for their health until it is gone. They are flying through life on a thread-bare rope–ready to snap.

If you are among the thousands who are seeking to win over some undesirable emotions such as anxiety, fear, frustration, guilt, anger, resentment, etc., you must not overlook the proper place of physical exercise in your strategy. It is a proven fact that exercise plays a vital role in winning over emotions, as it works its rejuvenatory magic–not by making us hurt–but by making us breathe and feel good. Dr. Theodore Klumpp (a medical consultant to the President's Council on Physical Fitness and Sports), said, "Staying active is the key to staying alive."

Some people like to make fun of exercise. We have all heard about the man who said, "Every time I get the desire to exercise, I lie down until it passes." Chauncey Depew, when asked if he took regular exercise, replied,

"I get my exercise acting as pallbearer to my friends who exercise." Even though he lived to be 94, I doubt that many of us will be able to follow the advice of Mr. Depew. The only exercise some people get is jumping to conclusion, running down their friends, sidestepping responsibility, pushing their luck, and racing their imaginations.

Mary called her minister one day as the last resort. "You must help me! I'm so depressed I could scream," she cried to him over the phone. Upon visiting Mary, he learned that she had not gone out of the house in two weeks; and that there wasn't anything wrong with her physically, according to her recent medical checkup. Her emotions were controlling her. She was reading her Bible and praying but that wasn't helping.

Mary's minister recognized a possible missing ingredient in her approach to winning over anxiety and depression. She needed physical activity. Upon her minister's insistence she began to walk around the block three times each day, once after each meal. In two weeks she attended church with a smile on her face telling everyone how great she was feeling. Physical exercise helped her win over emotions which were out of control.

EXPERTS AGREE ON BENEFITS OF EXERCISE

I have always been an advocate of proper exercise and diet. Presently my schedule calls for a seven mile run, three times a week, and a workout with weights two times per week. I feel great! I don't claim, however, to be an expert in the field of health or exercise. This is why I have collected the following research to prove my point relative to the importance of exercise.

Many people are not convinced that exercise is important. A few years back the Opinion Research Corporation of Princeton, N. J., conducted a survey that concluded that forty-nine million American adults do not engage in physical activity for the purpose of exercise. "Sedentary

Americans who don't exercise," says the Opinion report, "tend to be older, less well educated and less affluent than those who do exercise."

Why don't 49 million American adults exercise? How about you, do you have a regular exercise program? Notice some popular excuses given by people who don't exercise.

1. The majority of people believe they get enough exercise through their normal daily activities.

2. Many believe exercise is dangerous, or hard on the heart.

3. Some fear wearing themselves out through exercise.

4. Many claim they don't have time to exercise.

5. A few feel like exercise is a fad for the well-to-do.

6. Some don't bother with exercise when they are feeling okay.

7. Many shun it because of bad memories from gym class in school.

8. Some won't exercise because they believe everybody gets old and dies whether they exercise or not.

9. Some are just too lazy.

10. Some are ignorant of the benefits of exercise and thus refrain from it.

Dr. Richard Cabot, former professor of medicine and social ethics at Harvard University, in his book entitled *What Men Live By*, diagnosed man's emotional needs into four basic categories: 1) work, 2) play, 3) love, and 4) worship. If these areas are not properly balanced man will suffer. Work is doing that which you have to do. Play is doing something you don't have to do. Love is what every person must give and receive. Worship occurs when man's life is right with God. Exercise fits into categories one and two, but especially in two: PLAY. The challenge for many Christians is to stop being workaholics. "Possibly the greatest malaise in our country today," stated William McNamara, "is our neurotic compulsion to work." We must learn to relax and find time for exercise. This is a must for sound emotional health and physical well being.

Dr. Simonton has documented the role that exercise plays in his therapy for patients: "Exercise has more than physical benefits; it can produce significant psychological changes as well. Several studies have observed that people on regular exercise programs (specifically, a combination of walking and jogging) tend to be more flexible in their thinking and beliefs, they tend to have an increased sense of self-sufficiency, a strengthened self-concept, improved self-acceptance, less tendency to blame others, and less depression. The overall picture is that people engaged in regular exercise programs tend to develop a healthier psychological profile in general. . . . If exercise can help bring about physical changes in your immune system and the psychological attitude that contributes to your quality of life and possibly even your recovery, then establishing a regular program of exercise will be well worth it."

Dr. O. Quentin Hyder, M. D., in his book *Shape Up*, lists the following physiological benefits of exercise:

1. Better cardiovascular efficiency.
2. Lower blood pressure.
3. Lower serum cholesterol.
4. Higher ratio of high-density lipaprotein.
5. Increased coronary circulation.
6. Reduction of excess body fat.

7. Increased muscle size and strength (enabling the heart, for example, to pump more blood per beat).

8. Increased ability to consume oxygen.

Nathan Pritikin gives a number of benefits from exercise: "In addition to longterm benefits, such as building your resistance to heart disease and other cardiovascular and degenerative diseases, exercise gives you important bonuses that will make everyday living *right now* much more enjoyable. Decrease in stress is one bonus. Many people depend on drug therapy to relax; regular aerobic exercise provides a natural tranquilizer that reduces stress and anxiety. . . . People who exercise regularly tend to sleep better and deal more effectively with the conflicts of daily living. . . . Another bonus you'll discover is lessened fatigue. . . . There's really nothing like regular aerobic exercising to give you a sense of well being–and help you lose pounds and keep your weight where you want it to be after you have reached your goal."

Bruce Tulloh writes: "Through becoming fitter you become able to operate on a higher plane; thus at any given level the relative stress on your system is lessened . . . the benefits in terms of the decrease in tension after exercise have been measured and have been shown to be real."

The authors of *Type A Behavior And Your Heart* wrote: "Right from the outset, we wish you to know that we believe, as every physician we have ever known believes, that physical activity of the proper kind and amount is an eminently salutary adjunct of a well-balanced life . . . physical indolence has increased at about the same rate as the incidence of coronary heart disease in America, it is deeply suspect as a possible cause agent."

After a brief discussion of how sports and exercise help vent aggressiveness, McQuade and Aikman, in their book *Stress*, state: "But exercise is useful in another way, too. It not only dispels one form of stress in our lives, it also enables us to bear up better against stress in general. An engineering analogy comes to mind. Structural engineers in the past fifty years have learned, before assembling buildings and bridges, to pretest parts of them by applying preliminary loadings against the eventual anticipated loads that will come when the structures are completed and in use. Conditioning the body can accomplish the same kind of thing. A person who is in good physical condition will withstand the assault of a virus, or a spell of overwork—or even a quarrel with the foreman—better than someone who isn't. . . . Health aside, being in good physical shape is, of course, quite simply very pleasant—indeed, somewhat blissful."

The evidence is clear. Proper exercise improves your emotional health. It is better to work off anxieties, tensions and frustrations through a good exercise program than to take tranquilizers. Regardless of what you may think, exercise is very essential to your daily living. Exercise is the missing ingredient in most programs for winning over emotions.

There have been many, many times when I have come home with that tense, uptight feeling because of a busy schedule. After my run I feel like doing another 8 to 10 hours of work. The mental and physical boost it gives me is more than worth the time and effort put into the run.

PRINCIPLES FROM THE BIBLE

A healthy soul and a healthy body go together. John told Gauis: "I wish above all things that thou mayest prosper and be in health, even as thy soul prospereth" (III John 2). We must remember that our bodies are made from dust, and not of steel (cf. Psalm 103:14). Our bodies are like an elevator—they can only carry so much stress and strain. There is a load limit, and if the body is not conditioned to bear up under it, chances are it will break.

The body is called the temple of God (cf. I Corinthians 6:19, 20). Just as smoking, drinking, gluttony, etc., can harm the body, a lack of physical fitness (exercise) may also harm the body. Paul commands us to, ". . . therefore glorify God in your body . . ." (vs. 20). A neglected, uncared for body will not do this. In principle, Paul warns us about the serious consequences of harming God's temple, "If any man defile the temple of God, him shall God destroy; for the temple of God is holy, which temple ye are" (I Corinthians 3:17).

Many people never take into consideration the fact that Christ led a life of physical activity, instead of a sedentary one. As a teacher He could have stayed in the temple, or in a synagogue and let the people come to Him. He didn't! Our Savior was out on the roads, in the fresh air, walking from town to town (cf. Mark 1:38). He had few comforts as He moved about among the people. On one occasion, after a lot of work, the Master said, ". . . Come ye yourself apart into a desert place, and rest a while: for there were many coming and going, and they had no leisure so much as to eat" (Mark 6:31). The Lord recognized the need to get away and relax. Can we do less?

I believe we are safe in saying that Peter and the other disciples were hard workers. As a fisherman, Peter, had to wrestle with nets from early morning until late in the afternoon. Peter even sprinted to the empty tomb of Jesus: "So they ran both together: and the other disciple did outrun Peter, and came first to the sepulchre" (John 20:4).

Since we don't all have the opportunity to be fishermen, or workers in trades that demand hard physical labor, we must provide time and opportunities for our bodies to get some exercise. According to Paul, physical exercise is of some value (cf. I Timothy 4:8). As children of God we need to recognize this and make it part of our lifestyle. In our consumer oriented world we must be more vigorous in body. If we are not careful we will become sluggish in mind and body, always looking for the path of least resistance. A "great-to-be-alive" feeling comes over the body after it has gone through a period of vigorous exercise that involves high oxygen intake. Many of our aches and pains, which are sometimes brought about by tension, will leave when we get "the old blood flowing." It has been rightly said, "People who cannot find time for recreation are obligated sooner or later to find time for illness."

Jesus was a man who was under pressure. He knew what grief and suffering were all about. At times he had to flee to save His life. And yet in spite of all this, he was a man who possessed perfect peace. His weapon was trust in the Father and constant contact through prayer. He knew when to get away from the people. Thus, he left us an example that we should follow. It's okay to exercise the temple of God!

SOME BENEFICIAL EXERCISES

As a word of caution, it is unwise to rush out and begin a vigorous exercise program. I know by now you are sold on the benefits of exercise relative to its value to emotional well being. Let me suggest the following things before you begin. First, it is suggested by most physicians that a person have a thorough physical examination before engaging in a physical fitness program. Second, after the doctor gives the okay, look around for a good exercise program which is aerobic in nature. In conjunction with this I highly recommend that you read these two books: *The New Aerobics*, by Dr. Kenneth H. Cooper, M.D., and *Fat or Fit*, by Covert Bailey. Notice what Bailey has to say about the benefits of aerobic exercise: "Aerobic exercises are unquestionably the most *efficient* exercises to improve physical fitness. You will show greater improvement with aerobics, *per time spent*, than with any other exercise. Therefore, unless you have lots and lots of time to spend exercising, save tennis games, handball, skiing, weight lifting, or golf for fun and do aerobics for exercise.

An aerobic exercise is one which:

1. Is steady and nonstop.
2. Lasts a minimum of 12 minutes.
3. Maintains your heart at 70-80 percent of maximum for the entire time you are exercising.
4. Should be done a minimum of four days per week.

The following exercises qualify as aerobic:

1. Walking
2. Jogging
3. Running
4. Jumping rope
5. Bicycling (actual or stationary)
6. Rowing
7. Roller skating, ice skating
8. Cross-country skiing
9. Swimming
10. Rebounder (mini-trampoline)
11. Jumping Jacks
12. Chair stepping
13. Treadmill
14. Running in place

A WORD ABOUT DIET

Along with a good physical fitness program you must be careful about your diet. The kind of fuel you put into your body is very important. Good eating habits are essential for good health. I personally think the Book of Daniel (1:12-15) gives us an excellent illustration of the superiority of vegetables and water over rich, fat or junk foods. In Leviticus 3:17 Israel was warned about eating animal fat. Some basic guidelines for proper eating are as follows:

1. Be sure to eat a balanced diet from the basic food groups: dairy products, meat, fruits and vegetables, grains and breads. There are a number of good books in this area that you should read.

2. Stay, as much as possible, away from refined sugar, and avoid eating too much meat. Try as much as possible to eat your food as close to nature as possible. Our refining processes are destroying the food value of many products we consume.

3. I would like to also encourage you to eliminate the use of caffeine, or too much of it. Basically it has no food value and only plays havoc with the nerves.

4. Take plenty of time to eat your meals. Chew slowly and really taste the food (try to chew each bite 25 or more times).

5. If needed, take a good vitamin and mineral supplement.

6. Drink a lot of water each day (some persons drink eight glasses per day).

7. Use common sense in selecting your food. You don't have to have a second helping.

CONCLUSION

A good exercise program will help you feel good. When you feel good you are in a better frame of mind. When you are in a better frame of mind, you are able to win over your emotions with greater ease.

I once read that Dale Carnegie conducted a survey in which he asked what people were most interested in. The two major answers were: How to keep healthy, and how to have friends. Good health is a prized possession. Without it, all other things we own lose their value and excitement.

When you are physically fit your strength and resistance are high. Your body has a bounce and your face has a glow. Your nerves are calm. You are able to stand more stress, strain and pressure in your daily life. As the people gripe, blow their horns, have gnawing stomachs, worry and fret, you win over these emotional frustrations because your body is fit. Your happy mental outlook makes the difference.

Take some time right now to sit down and examine your total health patterns. Check every part of your being, see where you have been taking shortcuts or neglecting your physical man; discover where you can improve. Have you been neglecting your exercise program?

FOR THOUGHT AND DISCUSSION

1. Discuss I Timothy 4:8.
2. What was your initial reaction to this lesson on physical exercise?
3. Why do some people resent exercise?
4. Do you have an exercise program?
5. Do you know of a case where exercise helped a person with emotional problems?
6. Discuss what the experts say about the benefits of exercise.
7. Why don't 49 million American adults exercise?
8. Discuss man's four emotional needs.
9. Why does exercise have more than physical benefits?
10. Discuss III John 2.
11. Discuss the physical life of Christ and His disciples.
12. What is aerobic exercise?
13. How do you plan to use this lesson?
14. How is your diet? Discuss.
15. Share any additional comments or questions you may have.

CHAPTER SEVEN

WINNING OVER FEAR

"Let not your heart be troubled; ye believe in God, believe also in me" (John 14:1).

INTRODUCTION

A group of 100 college students were asked to list their fears. The group produced a list of over 500 fears. How about you–how many fears do you have on your list? If you are like most people, you have several items on your list. Fear is a major enemy of emotional well being. It seeks to destroy our peace of mind.

I once read about a man who saw a snake and at the same moment he was pricked by a barbed wire. Thinking he was bitten by the snake, he foamed at the mouth and acted as though he was dying. When a doctor arrived and saw there was no swelling at the abrasion, he assured the man that he had not been bitten. The man became well almost instantly. This is a classic example of the power of fear. I am sure you know of many such stories.

A physician once said, "The most common and the most subtle of all human diseases is fear." A person can be scared to death. Roosevelt was certainly right when he said, "The only thing we have to fear is fear itself." Why? Because of the destruction and unrest it brings.

THE BIBLE AND FEAR

"Well, isn't fear commanded in the Bible?" is the way a Christian responded to an admonition to reject fearfulness. Yes, fear is commanded in the Bible (cf. Proverbs 1:7; 9:10; 22:4). The fear, however, we are discussing in this lesson is the kind Paul talks about in II Timothy 1:7. The apostle wrote, "For God gave us NOT a spirit of fearfulness; but of power and love and discipline."

There are several Greek words that are translated *fear* in our English versions of the Bible. The basic word is *phobos*. This word denotes, among its several meanings, respect and reverential fear of God (e. g., Romans 8:15; Acts 9:31; Ephesians 5:31). *Phobos* is not the word used in II Timothy 1:7.

The word used in II Timothy by Paul is *deilia*. *Deilia* denotes moral cowardice and timidity and is never used in a good sense. It is an inward sensation of fear. This, for example, is the kind of fear within the hearts of the disciples when a great tempest arose on the sea of Galilee (Matthew 8:23-26). The fear of circumstances, and the fear of men, or the unknown, often makes a person a coward. Fear (respect) of God makes the righteous as bold as a lion–not a coward.

The adjective form of *deilia* is used in Revelation 21:8. This verse states that "the fearful will be cast into the lake of fire and brimstone." Fearfulness, therefore, is a serious matter and must be delt with by every person. Peace does not exist where there is a "spirit of fear."

NOT ALL FEAR IS BAD

I remember how excited I was when it became possible for me to become a boy scout. It seemed like I waited forever for that time to come. In rural Georgia it was one of the few things a boy could do. I will never forget the night I returned home from my first scout meeting. I got off the bus on the main highway; after this I had to walk over a mile down a dirt road to my house. It must have been the darkest night of the year. But, I was going to be brave; after all, I was now a scout. After going about 200 yards down the road I started to imagine all sorts of things; my thoughts began to run wild. My heart was pounding and my feet began to run. I am sure I broke the four minute mile that night! As I ran I thought of "101 things" that could get me; why only a year before some men had broken out of jail. My emotions pushed the fear button and I responded accordingly. I laugh at it now. But I can assure you it wasn't a laughing matter that night. Montaigne was right when he said, "Fear sometimes adds wings to the heels, and sometimes nails them to the ground, and fetters them from moving."

I am sure you have many little stories like this one. Such stories remind us that a certain amount of fear was necessary for our growing up. Likewise, it still has a place in our world as adults.

Fear, as a basic human emotion, is not wrong per se. God has created man with the ability to regard certain dangers with protective fear. This is for man's preservation and safety. If a barking dog jumps at you, the feeling of fright which comes into your heart is natural. It will motivate you to do what is necessary to avoid harm by the dog. As part of their growth training, children must be taught the dangers of playing in a busy street. Through healthy fear (and respect) for cars they will avoid foolish actions which may lead to harm.

We must be careful, however, not to let the reasonable fears turn into destroyers of our peace of mind. Sometimes we are like a royal Bengal tiger I read about. The caged tiger exhibited a great terror at the sight of a rat. If the rat moved about, the tiger ran or sprang away, as if it was afraid of the destruction. A drop of the paw would have crushed his enemy; but fear caused the tiger to miss the fact. We must not let the "little mice" destroy our peace of mind.

Fear, as a natural emotion, can be constructive in our day to day living. If you hear the cry, "Fire!", rest assured that your mind will push the fear button and you will depart quickly. The challenge is not to panic and hurt others in your efforts to escape. Knowing when to listen to fear is a vital key to successful living. Warning our children about busy streets and the dangers of being hit by a car is okay. In time this infantile fear will be replaced by mature common sense. Also, when it comes to discipline, the fear of punishment is a positive motivation for good.

WHAT ARE YOU AFRAID OF?

What is your answer to this question? Some answers that are regularly given are as follows:

1. *Fear of failure.* Some persons are afraid to try a new venture because they don't want to fail. Certainly no one wants to fail, but a few failures along life's road are normal.

2. *Fear of criticism.* Some people are so concerned with what others think, that they never attempt a new challenge. "What will . . . think?" is the chain that keeps them from becoming creative doers, etc.

3. *Fear of rejection.* Joe wanted to play football. But he was afraid to go for the tryouts because of the fear of rejection. I know a man in his late forties who is afraid to ask women for dates because he fears rejection (he is single and never has been married).

4. *Fear of authority.* Some people panic when they are approached by a person of authority. This may be the boss, a policeman, or some other person.

5. *Fear of death.* At one time or another the fear of death comes into everyone's heart. Some people, however, live in a constant fear of death. They torture themselves day after day with this fear.

6. *Fear of national disaster.* Scores of people across our land live in a deep fear of war, riots, etc. I have met many who worry about the fact that I live in California.

Why? Because they believe someday we will fall into the ocean (as a land mass).

7. *Fear of success.* This is an avoidance motive. Such thinking believes that success will have negative consequences, disappointment, rejection, and even abandonment if we achieve it.

8. *Fear of things going too well.* I have heard persons say, "Things are going too well, something bad is about to happen." They can't enjoy the sun for expecting the clouds. Just around the next bend in the road their luck will run out.

9. *Fear of loss.* Thousands are working their 9 to 5 jobs, as well as other hours, with a deep fear of losing their jobs. This is especially true of persons who are close to retirement age. Others fear the loss of friends, respect, property, money, health, approval, and a host of other things.

10. *Fear of openness.* This person will never let you see behind his/her mask. They are afraid to reveal the real self. One person recently said, "If you knew the real me, you wouldn't like me."

11. *Fear of problems.* I know a church leader who believes in "peace at all cost." This man can't cope with anything that might produce a problem.

12. *Fear of the unknown.* This challenges all of us from time to time. I know some persons, however, who will not try a new restaurant, go to a new place for a vacation, change make of cars, etc., because they fear the unknown.

13. *Fear of change.* This is produced in a number of situations. Some people eat the same food week after

week; others wear the same brand of clothes over and over; some wear the same hair style. Some people can't stand to get out of their self-imposed comfort zone.

14. *Fear of the past.* This is a form of guilt that people live with. They live with dread that the past will, in some way, harm them. Others are afraid of the future, because it is unknown.

15. *Fear of punishment.* This takes on many forms. Some live in fear of hell because of God's wrath. Others are afraid of being falsely accused of something they didn't do.

16. *Fear of a deadly disease.* Some people live in fear of cancer, heart trouble and a host of other diseases. Some day, at some time, they don't really know when, one of these enemies will strike them.

17. *Fear of old age.* Every where we look today we are reminded that youth is in, and old age is out. The suicide rate for retired men is twelve times that of those who are employed. I like the sign that General Douglas MacArthur is reported to have had over his desk: "Youth is not a time of life—it is a state of mind."

18. *Phobias.* Millions of people are possessed by phobias. A phobia is a fear of some object, situation, place or thing which, in itself, poses no actual danger to the person. A person with a phobia usually knows that his fear is irrational, but he can't seem to do anything about it. The following are some common fears (phobias) which trouble people:

a. Fear of high places (acrophobia).
b. Fear of public places (agoraphobia).
c. Fear of thunder, lightning or storms (astraphobia).

d. Fear of closed places (claustrophobia).
e. Fear of water (hydrophobia).
f. Fear of solitude (monophobia).
g. Fear of darkness (night) (nyctophobia).
h. Fear of crowds (ochlophobia).
i. Fear of disease (pathophobia).
j. Fear of death (thanatophobia).

Persons with such fears will do about anything to avoid the objects of their phobias. Their fear may range from mild to very serious anxiety. They may have physical symptoms such as nausea, dizziness, backaches, headaches, skin rashes, fainting spells, and other pains.

WHY AM I AFRAID?

Mary, a happily married mother of two, could not understand why she was so afraid of dogs. Her children wanted one for a pet. It didn't matter how small or large the dog was, she was afraid of it. The dog may have gone through obedience school, or have been house broken, she didn't want the animal.

Through help from a family counselor, Mary discovered why she was afraid of dogs. When she was a child, a neighborhood dog had attacked her brother. For years the scene of his bleeding legs stayed in her mind. This is why any time she would come near a dog she would react with deep anxiety and fear. After coming to grips with this truth, Mary won over her fear of dogs. The children now have two dogs.

Some causes of fear aren't as easy to locate as this one. But one thing is certain: All fear, unless there is an organic illness, is the product of my emotional self. Whether I push the fear button because of parental influences, displacement anxiety, repressed impulses, guilty conscience, ignorance, feelings of weakness, or unbelief, I am responsible for my fear. The challenge, therefore, is for me to be honest with myself; confront my fear; and invite God to help me win over it.

KEYS TO WINNING

Since God wants us to win over fear, it is essential for us to develop a game plan. Since fear is a complicated and individual thing, it is obvious that there is no one quick cure for all our fears. The following keys will help you win over fear.

First, you must believe you can win over fear. This is the starting place. Fear cannot win over you! Napoleon once said, "He who fears being conquered is sure of defeat."

Second, you must admit the existence of the fear. This is not easy because it goes against our pride. Therefore, it will require honesty, personal examination and courage on your part. Fearfulness will never be removed without this step.

Third, name the fear. Don't use the nebulous, "I am afraid." Be specific! You can't win over an enemy if you don't know its name.

Fourth, try to recognize its origin. It is not from God! He hasn't given you a spirit of fear (cf. II Timothy 1:7). It, therefore, comes from other sources; i. e., wrong thinking, the flesh, the evil one, etc.

Fifth, confess it to God. Don't be afraid or ashamed to say, "Father, I am afraid to stand before the Bible class," etc. Also, it may have become a sinful condition that needs to be confessed to the Father. Always be honest with God.

Sixth, check your love quotient. John wrote, "There is no fear in love; but perfect love casteth out fear: because fear hath torment. He that feareth is not made perfect in love" (I John 4:18).

Seventh, do what you fear. This will be very difficult. But in some cases it is the final step to winning over the fear.

Eighth, ask yourself, "What happened the last time I had this fear?" I am sure you will discover the answer will be, "Nothing." That which you feared went on its way until you called it up again.

Ninth, work on developing your faith. We must trust God and His word. When we fill up on faith, fear doesn't have a chance. Fear and faith do not mix!

Tenth, separate the feeling of fear from the object of fear. This will usually prove to us that our fear is the product of our thinking. This will help you recognize fear as an emotion you can handle.

Eleventh, pray for strength to defeat this foe. James promises us that God will answer prayers prayed in faith (cf. James 1:5-7).

Twelfth, resolve on a daily basis to reject fearfulness. Some psychologists believe that in order to acquire a new habit, a person must practice it a minimum of 21 times before it becomes part of his subconscious and thus productive in daily living. You must be persistent in your attack on fear.

Thirteenth, claim God's power. It is given to Christians to defeat the evil one, and to live the victorious life in Christ (cf. Ephesians 3:20; Revelation 12:10; II Tim. 1:7).

Fourteenth, be a disciplined person. This is also in our text of II Timothy 1:7. We are in control of what we think and do (cf. Proverbs 23:7). We don't have to let the spirit of fear into our hearts and minds.

Fifteenth, turn to others for help. Paul admonishes us to "bear one another's burdens" (Galatians 6:1, 2). This is one of the blessings of being in a spiritual family. We can get help when we need it.

Sixteenth, you may need to see a physician. If you suspect some organic or physical problem, your family doctor will be able to determine if this is the source of your fear. Be careful, however, of tranquilizers, depressants and psychic energizers as cures for your fear. Also, professional analysis by a qualified Christian physician may be an important step in reducing your fear.

CONCLUSION

Fear is a very real foe of the Christian's peace of mind. This foe is pervasive, powerful and complex. It does not come from God. This doesn't mean, however, that we can't win over it. We can! Through God's power and some simple principles, we can remove this enemy from our lives.

Fear also has a legitimate purpose. It serves as an alerting mechanism that causes us to take action to protect ourselves from all kinds of dangers. This fear releases emotional energy which helps us respond ("flight") in an appropriate way. God created us with this ability.

Our goal is to win over the negative fears that make spiritual cowards out of us. Fear must be won over because it can arouse other negative emotions such as anger, hatred, depression, frustration, and a host of others.

As we win over fear, THE BEST IS YET TO BE!

FOR THOUGHT AND DISCUSSION

1. Give a good illustration of fear.
2. Can a person be scared to death? Discuss.
3. How is fear misunderstood?
4. Discuss II Timothy 1:7.
5. What kind of fear is approved in the Bible?
6. Define fear.

7. How is fear natural? Discuss.
8. What are you afraid of?
9. What is a phobia?
10. Do you have any phobias? Discuss.
11. What causes fear?
12. Discuss keys to winning over fear.
13. How do you plan to use this lesson?
14. Share some additional points.
15. Have you read any good books dealing with fear? Share.

CHAPTER EIGHT

WINNING OVER GUILT

"Some people still feel guilty after they have been pronounced innocent."

INTRODUCTION

It was a hot July day in Louisiana. The humidity and temperature both stood at 100 degrees. It seems like it was only yesterday, but in reality it was over thirteen years ago, when I walked upon the front porch and approached the old man sitting in his rocking chair. I was door-knocking in a gospel campaign and this house was on my list of streets to cover. His tanned, weather-beaten face and calloused hands revealed the toll of many hard years of work. His eyes were sad and revealed a loneliness. He was very warm and friendly.

After discussing the weather and a lot of other small talk subjects, we finally got around to talking about Christ and the Bible. During our discussion of God's love the old man started to cry. He said, sadly, "I can't be saved!"

"Why?" I asked (in a voice of surprise).

"During the war I killed several men; about thirty years ago a preacher told me that I had committed the unpardonable sin. There is no use wasting your time on me."

After spending another hour with him discussing God's grace, love and forgiveness, as well as how God forgave Paul of murder, I left the old man with a ray of hope. "How sad," I thought, as I walked away, "for thirty years he has been carrying the guilt of committing the unpardonable sin because a preacher taught him wrong."

Guilt is one of the strongest robbers of peace. It

stalks the minds of men and women trying to take away their happiness and emotional stability.

"I just can't forgive myself! I am to blame for my daughter getting pregnant. It was something I did . . . or didn't do . . .," is how a weeping mother expressed her feelings of guilt to me in a counseling session. Her only child, who was raised attending church, was pregnant and not married. This fine Christian mother is just one of millions who hold themselves guilty for the actions of their children.

These two illustrations are not isolated cases of guilt. Millions are suffering with the emotional pains of guilt on a daily basis. Some of these people are actually guilty; others are suffering from neurotic or self-imposed guilt. In either case the result is the same: *loss of peace and happiness.*

It has been stated that most people are harboring some form of guilt in the inner chambers of their souls. What would you do if you received a note like this one: "Fly at once, all is discovered." It is reported that Sir Arthur Doyle sent this note to twelve of his friends as a practical joke. Within twenty-four hours all twelve of the famous men had left the country. Why did they flee? Was it merely a coincidence? Evidently they all had guilty consciences. Looming over the heads of most persons is a dark cloud of guilt which they try to hide, deny, run from, or camouflage. Shakespeare wrote, "The mind of the guilty is filled with scorpions."

DEFINING GUILT

In our study of winning over guilt it is necessary to define the term and to note the different kinds of guilt.

1. Webster defines guilt as: 1) "The art or state of having done a wrong or committed an offense. 2) conduct that involves guilt; crime or sin."

2. Dr. Clyde M. Narramore defines guilt as: "Guilt may be defined as feeling sinfulness, evil, wrong-doing and failure to measure up."

3. Dr. Wayne Dyer gives this practical definition: "Guilt means that you use up your present moments being immobilized as a result of *past* behavior, while worry is the contrivance that keeps you immobilized in the now about something in the *future*—frequently something over which you have no control."

Guilt is a product of the mind which occurs when a person realizes that he has violated moral, religious or ethical standards (i.e., rules, laws, principles, etc.). With the realization that one has done wrong comes guilt and a regretful or sorrowful feeling which decreases your feelings of personal worth and peace of mind. The guilt may be real or imagined; as a result the victim suffers mental torment and unhappiness. From one case of wrong the domino affect occurs: one wrong thought sets off another wrong thought and on and on it goes until the person is emotionally ruined. It is at this point that thousands turn to strong drink, drugs, or suicide in an effort to escape the pangs of guilt.

This lesson is dealing basically with subjective or self-imposed guilt. Some guilty feelings are healthy because they lead us to get our lives right with God and our fellow man. Most guilt, however, is unhealthy because it is neurotic and unrealistic. Thus, when we speak of a guilt complex we are usually talking about unhealthy guilt which is self-induced. This is very difficult to deal with in some cases. It is safe to say that any form of guilt that cannot be traced to the violation of some proper standard is neurotic in nature. The neurotic person lives with his guilt burden as a way of life. The smallest thing will set it off and send him into deep depression. It is also true that some neurotic guilt may stem from a real guilt that has not been properly delt with. The person who is feeling guilty should always ask himself these two questions:

1. Why do I feel guilty?
2. What valid standard (rule) have I violated?

The answers should help him pinpoint whether his guilt is objective or subjective: real or imagined. Having answered these two questions, as well as learned the source of his guilt, a person is in a better position to win over his guilt.

ORIGIN OF GUILT

It is too simple to state that guilt is the product of man's mind or conscience. Additional insight must be gained in order to effectively handle this emotion. A person's personality is involved in creating guilt, as well as every negative and positive thing that he has come in contact with. Man is affected by every experience he has had. This goes all the way back to childhood. The adult is the continuation of the child. Behavioral psychologists tell us that the most important time of psychic growth occurs during the first five to seven years of life. The influences that shape our personalities help us understand why some persons have more guilt than others, or why some feel guilty while others don't. For example some people may murder another person and not feel guilty, and others will feel guilty for running over a dog.

Any study of guilt from a Biblical standpoint presupposes that God created man with a conscience. At birth it is free from guilt and distortions. During childhood growth it develops rapidly and continues to develop throughout life. On any given day a person's conscience is the result of what has been programmed into it. In addition to the fact that our conscience is a product of birth and early childhood training, and helps develop guilty feelings, the following things also contribute to feelings of guilt.

1. Thinking you have done something wrong may lead to guilt. There may be no evidence to support your thoughts but you still think that you are a "bad person." This is distorted thinking.

2. A poor self-image usually leads to guilt feelings. Many psychologists believe that all inferiority is the result of guilt experiences.

3. Perfectionist attitude. Mary thought she should be happy all the time. On the days she felt sad or down she felt very guilty.

4. Unrealistic expectations lead to guilt feelings. Parents, if they are not careful, will set standards for their children which are too high or unreasonable. The child may be a B student and the parents keep pushing for an A. Guilt comes because standards are impossible to reach.

5. False conscience development produces guilt. This is the popular "Let your conscience be your guide" philosophy of life. Some people call right wrong and wrong right.

6. Actual guilt which is produced by a healthy conscience given by God to help men shun the wrong and do the right. The Bible says that on one occasion some people who heard Jesus were convicted by their own conscience (cf. John 8:9). In many cases people feel guilty because they are guilty! This is objective guilt.

We have all grown up with certain values programmed into our minds. These are the "shalls and shall nots"; the "do this and don't do that"; the "please and will you" commands. From all this we developed our sense of right and wrong. Guilt comes from inner feelings of remorse and self-condemnation because of our actions. One young lady put it this way, "When I go dancing I feel guilty because my parents taught me it was wrong." This is objective guilt.

Jerry felt guilty about being in college. He could still hear the words of his mother, "You are leaving home because you don't love me." This is subjective guilt.

VARIOUS KINDS OF GUILT

Guilt comes from many sources. Notice some of the following producers of objective guilt.

1. *Personal guilt.* This is the result of violating your own personal standard. A person may feel guilty if he cuts down on his work to spend some time with his family. He feels guilty the whole time he is having fun.

2. *Legal guilt.* This occurs when a person violates one of the laws of the community. A good example is running a red light, or some other law violation.

3. *Social guilt.* This occurs for example when a person wears the wrong kind of dress to a party, or has poor manners for the occasion. She feels out of place and feelings of guilt or remorse come over her.

4. *National guilt.* Some people feel guilty because they have bought an imported car. They feel like they are causing the inflation in our country. Some politicians major in guilt tactics in their speeches.

5. *Institutional guilt.* Some companies make employees feel guilty if they won't support a certain policy, or back them on a certain move, etc. One man recently said, "My old alma mater is trying to raise money by hanging a guilt trip on me. It won't work!"

6. *Religious guilt.* This occurs when you violate

the standards of an organized group, or fail to take part in certain activities, etc., which may or may not be authorized by the Bible. A mother of three small children told me recently, "I feel so guilty because I can't take part in all the activities that the other women are doing."

7. *Sin guilt.* This occurs when a person violates a divine standard given by God. This is at the base of most of the guilt in our society. When the sin problem is eliminated the guilt problem usually goes too. Read Romans 1:14-32.

A person may do all of the seven things listed above and not feel guilty. It depends upon what he has done with his conscience. Paul wrote: "Now the Spirit speaketh expressly, that in latter times some shall depart from the faith, giving heed to seducing spirits, and doctrines of devils; speaking lies in hypocrisy, having their conscience seared with a hot iron" (I Timothy 4:1, 2).

THE BIBLE AND GUILT

Paul makes it clear that because of sin all the world is guilty before God (Romans 3:19, 23). Sin is a violation of God's law and leads to separation from Jehovah (Isaiah 59:1, 2; I John 5:17; 3:4). Since man is guilty of sin, therefore, it is not wrong for him to feel guilty. This is why he needs an atonement for his sin: to take away his condemnation so that he may appear before God justified.

There are many examples in the Bible of persons experiencing guilt. Study very carefully the following examples.

1. Adam and Eve hide themselves in the garden because they felt the guilt of their sin (cf. Genesis 3:7-13).

2. The sons of Jacob: "They said one to another, We are verily guilty concerning our brother, in that we saw

the anguish of his soul, when he besought us, and we would not hear; therefore is this distress come upon us" (Genesis 42:21).

3. King David knew the pangs of guilt. The book of Psalms contains many of his inner feelings of remorse. David said: "Have mercy upon me, O God, according to thy lovingkindness: according unto the multitude of thy tender mercies blot out my transgressions. Wash me throughly from mine iniquity, and cleanse me from my sin. For I acknowledge my transgression: and my sin is ever before me" (Psalm 51:1-3).

4. Judas committed suicide because of guilt. "Then Judas, which had betrayed him, when he saw that he was condemned, repented himself, and brought again the thirty pieces of silver to the chief priests and elders, Saying I have sinned in that I have betrayed the innocent blood . . . and he departed, and went and hanged himself" (Matthew 27:3-5).

5. The Jews on the day of Pentecost felt guilty. They cried out when they were pricked in their hearts and asked, ". . . men and brethren what shall we do?" (Acts 2:37).

The psychologists and psychiatrists spend a lot of their time trying to help people handle their guilt. In most cases, however, these helpers fail to take in consideration that the guilt of sin is one of man's major problems. Until man's sin problem is Biblically handled, this statement by the prophet will always be true: "But the wicked are like the troubled sea, when it cannot rest, whose waters cast up mire and dirt. There is no peace, saith my God, to the wicked" (Isaiah 57:20, 21).

God's word not only gives us many examples and consequences of guilt, it also, as we shall see in detail later on, gives us the solution for real guilt. The blood of Christ is the answer to our sin and guilt problems.

RESULTS OF GUILT

The results of guilt are as varied as the persons who have the feelings. I do believe, however, that some of the major reactions to feelings of guilt are as follows. (As well as the others mentioned in this lesson):

1. *Self-condemnation.* When a person condemns himself because of guilt feelings, he is also opening the door for a host of other emotional problems such as loneliness, inferiority complex, anxiety. He usually feels that he is merely getting what he deserves for being so bad.

2. *Blame game.* A person who feels the pain of guilt, as a general rule, will try to place the blame on others for his problems and wrongs. At times he will even become angry when the other persons deny his charges.

3. *Pessimism.* It is hard for a person with a heavy load of guilt to have a positive attitude. Guilt usually causes a person to develop a negative outlook on life.

4. *Martyr complex.* This is produced by the person who not only thinks he is getting what he deserves but also believes things will always be this way.

5. *Physical illness.* A person can actually make himself sick through a failure to deal properly with the emotional aspects of guilt.

6. *Growth and change.* These are the positive and healthy aspects of guilt. These come through handling guilt God's way.

7. *Repentance and turning to God.* This is another positive benefit of guilt. Nothing is more important than getting one's life right with God. This is the basis of all right and happy living.

8. *Forgiveness.* The acceptance of this is the ultimate surgery for all guilt. First, it must come from God; second, if possible, from others; and third, from self.

THE CURE FOR GUILT

Over twenty years ago a psychologist name O. Hobart Mower wrote these words, "man sickens in mind, soul and perhaps even body because of unconfessed and unatoned real guilt." The unusual thing about this statement is that it comes from a man who doesn't profess to be a Christian; and yet, he recognizes the need for confession and forgiveness. It is also interesting to note that less than ten years ago, psychiatrist Karl Menninger expressed the same basic idea in his book entitled, *What Became of Sin?* It should also be noted that these men were not approaching confession and forgiveness from the Biblical perspective. It merely reminds us that others are just discovering what God has been saying all along.

From our study so far it has become clear that guilt can be a complicated emotion. Certain types of neurotic guilt may need the services of a professional counselor. Most subjective and objective guilt, however, can be helped through the use of the following suggestions.

1. Admit to yourself that you are experiencing guilt. Also, pinpoint how long you have been feeling guilty.

2. On paper write down specifically what you are feeling guilty about. Be very honest with yourself.

3. Examine the validity of the supposed standard you violated. Who set the standard?

4. Ask yourself, "Is this a carryover guilt from my youth?"

5. Is someone else trying to manipulate you? Who? Why do you suppose they are doing this? Are you responding as they want?

6. Remember that the past is behind you. It can only hurt you as you use it against yourself.

7. If you discover that you are actually guilty of a wrong then confess it to God. He is ready to forgive if you will confess (read I John 1:8, 9).

8. Repent of your wrong. Repent means to "change your mind." Jesus made this essential to forgiveness (cf. Luke 13:3, 5; cf. Acts 2:38).

9. Never doubt the power of Christ's blood that was shed for the remission of sins (cf. Matthew 26:28; Acts 20:28; Revelation 1:5).

10. Remember that God has promised to "remember our sins no more" (cf. Jeremiah 31:30-32). As far as the east is from the west that's how far he will remove our transgressions" (cf. Psalm 103:12).

11. Remember that after repentance and forgiveness there isn't anything you can do. Your feelings of guilt won't change the past.

12. Acknowledge that there may be some things that others don't like about you. It's their problem. You can't please everybody.

13. Remember your guilt feelings that arise after cleansing do not come from God.

14. Are you trying to accept someone else's burden?

15. You can remove any label you have placed on yourself (e.g., "I am a bad person").

16. Always try to deal with the real problem and not just the symptoms.

17. Remember this syllogism:

a. I am guilty because of sin.
b. The blood of Christ takes away sin.
c. Therefore, I am no longer condemned by my sin.

18. Meditate upon John 8:36: "If the Son therefore shall make you free, ye shall be free indeed." Believe this!

19. If you need to right a wrong with another person don't be afraid to do so.

20. Pray for wisdom to properly handle your guilt (cf. James 1:5).

21. Visualize the blood of Christ washing your sins away. Also, imagine you are in front of the Lord and hear Him make this pronouncement: "You are no longer condemned. Go and sin no more."

CONCLUSION

There is a story about the meanest man in a small town becoming a Christian. Every Sunday morning after church services the man would wait for the preacher so that he could ask him this question, "Do you mean they are all forgiven, preacher?" To which the preacher would reply, "Yes, Sam they are all forgiven!"

This continued for about a month. Then one morning when Sam asked the preacher the same question again, the preacher replied: "Sam, let me tell you for the last time. God, through Christ Jesus, has forgiven you of all your past sins. They have been washed away. This is what He tells us in His word. You are going to have to believe this, or just call Him a liar!"

Sam is like so many who find it almost too good to believe that God can take away all sin and its condemnation. This is the Good News message of the gospel. Jesus is the Lamb of God that takes away the sins of the world (cf. John 1:29; Luke 19:10).

The Biblical cure for guilt is confrontation. Confess it and repent of it and God will forgive you. The challenge is for you to accept His forgiveness, as well as to forgive yourself. Through the blood of Christ you can win over guilt (cf. I John 1:7).

FOR THOUGHT AND DISCUSSION

1. Why is guilt a serious problem in our society?
2. How does guilt rob us of peace?
3. Define guilt.
4. Have you ever struggled with guilt?
5. What is self-imposed guilt?
6. What is objective guilt?
7. What are some of the major causes of guilt?
8. Have you ever tried to help a person win over guilt? Discuss.
9. Discuss the most serious case of guilt you have ever seen.
10. Discuss the different kinds of guilt.
11. When should a person experience real guilt?
12. What are some of the results of guilt?
13. How do you plan to use this lesson?
14. Discuss cures for guilt.
15. Share additional points you may have on this subject.

CHAPTER NINE

WINNING OVER ANGER

"When angry, count to ten before you speak; if very angry, a hundred." (Thomas Jefferson)

INTRODUCTION

Marge had worked all day cleaning the house for the ladies meeting she was going to have the next morning. She had even scrubbed the carpet, a job normally reserved for her husband. Feeling very pleased with the accomplishments of the day, Marge sat in her kitchen drinking a much deserved cup of coffee. Suddenly the door popped open and in ran her nine-year-old son, Ted, who had been in school all day, chasing the family dog, Blackie. Marge couldn't believe her eyes as she sat frozen in her seat watching Ted chase Blackie through the living room, into the den and around and around the dining room table. After recovering from the initial shock of seeing the muddy tracks on her clean carpet, she exploded.

Bill had been waiting in line for over an hour to buy tickets for a concert. This was one event he didn't want to miss. Just as he was about to step up to the window and purchase his tickets, a man stepped in front of him and proceeded to place his order. Bill blew his cool and started shouting at the line breaker.

The local newspaper recently carried an account of a father who had beaten his infant son to death. The father's reason for doing it was because the child made him mad when he cried during the night.

A man was having his car filled with gas when the attendant started to use the name of the Lord in vain. "Please watch your language," the purchaser said, "I don't appreciate you talking about my heavenly Father!"

The emotion described in the above four illustrations is anger. Anger is sometimes a perfectly normal reaction; and on some occasions it can (and does) get out of hand and lead to serious (or sinful) actions. The challenge comes in how we handle our anger. Do you handle it correctly or does it rule you? Socrates, finding himself very mad at a slave, said, "I would beat you if I were not so angry."

Two boys, named Gus and Gene, were taking turns spinning a top. They had but one top, which they spun alternately. As time passed they began to quarrel and soon became angry. Gene said, "It is my turn to spin the top." Gus said, "You lie!" They started hitting each other in a great rage; and, in the fight, Gene took a knife from his pocket, and stabbed Gus, who died a few minutes later. One lost his life, the other became a murderer, merely to determine whose turn it was to spin the top.

Anger is not a laughing matter. It is a very serious emotion that must be properly understood and controlled.

WHAT IS ANGER?

Anger, like all emotions, is created by your thinking. Your thoughts push the anger button. It begins with an event that you notice and the interpretation you place on it. The result of your interpretation is feeling and feeling leads to emotional action (in this case anger). This, therefore, makes it very difficult to give a definite definition of anger.

Anger is the result of emotional frustration or hostility. Webster defines anger as, "a hostile feeling of displeasure that may result from injury, mistreatment, opposition." There are several words translated anger from the Greek: *Orge* (noun), "Originally any natural impulse, or desire, or disposition, came to signify anger, as the strongest of all passions" (cf. Ephesians 4:31;

Colossians 3:8; I Timothy 2:8; James 1:19, 20); *Thumos*, "indicates a more agitated condition of the feelings, an outburst of wrath from inward indignation, while *orge* suggests a more settled or abiding condition of mind, frequently with a view of taking revenge. *Orge* is less sudden in its rise than *thumos*. *Thumos* expresses more the inward feeling, *orge* the more active emotion. *Thumos* is translated *wrath*. *Origizo* (a verb), means "to provoke, to arouse to anger" (cf. Ephesians 4:26; Matthew 5:22; Luke 14:21; 15:28).

Anger occurs when our desires or purposes are blocked. The following words illustrate the various forms anger may take.

1. Anger may be *hidden*. Psychologists tell us that most anger is concealed within the heart of man. It is like a basketball submerged in water; sooner or later, if it is not properly handled, it will pop to the top.

2. Anger may take the form of a mild *annoyance*. It may upset you when a person pops his gum.

3. Anger may be a *short outburst* of *resentment*. You may resent it for a few moments when someone cuts in front of you on the freeway.

4. Anger may be carried as *hatred* in the heart. One man confessed that he had hated his Second Grade teacher for twenty years because she embarrassed him one time in class. He was angry then but couldn't do anything about it.

5. Anger sometimes takes on the form of *aggression*. People try to overthrow governments because they don't like their policies, etc. Children become bullies because of anger.

6. Anger can also manifest itself in *revenge*. A man let the air out of his neighbor's car tires because it was parked in his driveway.

7. Anger may be *explosive*. This was seen in the case of the man who went into a rage and killed his boss because he was fired from his job. *Rage* is very dangerous.

8. Anger is an *emotional capacity* given to each of us by God. Anger, by itself, is neither good or bad, it is how we handle it that makes the difference.

9. Anger sometimes is no more than a mild case of *irritation*. One lady confessed that she became irritated (angry) when the preacher went overtime in his sermon.

10. Not all anger is wrong or sinful. Paul wrote, "Be angry and sin not" (Ephesians 4:26). The challenge is to know when to stop.

Many years ago Henry W. Beecher wrote these fine remarks about the nature of anger: "There is an anger that is damnable; it is the anger of selfishness. There is an anger that is majestic as the frown of Jehovah's brow: it is the anger of truth and love. If a man meets with injustice, it is not required that he shall not be roused to meet it; but if he is angry after he has had time to think upon it, that is sinful. The flame is not wrong, but the coals are." Anger, under proper control, can be a very necessary reaction. It can be used as a tool of communication to let others know how we feel about their conduct. God gave us anger as an emotion for constructive purposes. It is only through His word and power that we can make the best usage of our anger.

THE BIBLE AND ANGER

As we have already noted, anger, in and of itself, is not bad or sinful. It is an emotion which we have the capacity to feel because of God's creative work (cf. Genesis 1:27-29). It was given for our good. This is why we must learn to properly control it.

The Bible gives us a lot of positive information in our study of winning over anger.

First, it may come as a surprise to learn that anger is an attribute of God. There are more than 500 references to anger and wrath in the Old Testament. The Bible reveals that God experiences daily anger because of the evil actions of man. The Psalmist wrote, "God judgeth the righteous, and God is angry with the wicked every day" (Psalm 7:11). The Creator of man is "emotionally" moved when His creation rebels against Him. We, too, should be moved by the ungodliness in the world. We must hate the sin and love the sinner (cf. John 3:16).

We must always remember that God's anger is free from malice, injustice, unethical and hasty qualities. Jehovah is not an impulsive judge. The divine anger is to be regarded as the natural expression of His nature, which is absolute holiness, manifesting itself against the rebellion of man. This is why Paul wrote, "For the wrath of God is revealed from heaven against all ungodliness and unrighteousness of men . . ." (Romans 1:28).

Second, there are many examples of uncontrolled anger in the Bible. Some of these are: (a) Cain became angry and murdered his brother (Genesis 4:3-12); (b) Esau resented Jacob for deceiving him (Genesis 27:41); (c) King Saul committed many sins because of his anger (read I Samuel 18:8 - 31:4); (d) Haman plotted murder because of his anger (Esther 3:5 - 7:10); (e) King Ahab hated the prophet Micaiah and sought revenge (I Kings 22:8-27); and (f) The Jews became furious at Jesus and began to develop a plan to destroy Him (Luke 6: 10, 11).

Third, the Bible commands us to properly handle our anger. Study carefully the following passages: (a) "Cease from anger, and forsake wrath; fret not thyself in any wise to do evil" (Psalm 37:8); (b) "Be not hasty in thy spirit to be angry; for anger resteth in the bosom of fools" (Ecclesiastes 7:9); (c) "A hot-tempered man stirs up dissension, but a patient man calms a quarrel" (Prov. 15:18); (d) "But I say to you that every one who is angry with his brother shall be liable to judgment . . ." (Matthew 5:22); and (e) "A hot-tempered man must pay the penalty; if you rescue him, you will have to do it again" (Proverbs 19:19).

Fourth, the Bible reveals that there is an approved place for proper anger. Jesus, the perfect Son of God, was moved with anger when He saw the money changers taking advantage of the poor (John 2:12-17). This "make-a-buck" approach to religion, with its huckstering of religion for profit, was more than the Master could tolerate. He was emotionally moved by the sight and made a whip of cords and drove them all out of the Temple. The disciples were surprised by His actions; then they remembered a passage from Psalm 69:9 where it was written, "Zeal for thy house consume me." The word *consume* refers to the intensity of holy zeal from within, as well as the actions it produced. Jesus experienced righteous anger because of the sin of the money changers. He moved, not because of hatred of the men, or because He needed to blow off steam, but because of their wrong actions. The Proverb writer said, "A fool gives full vent to his anger, but a wise man, holding it back quiets it" (Proverbs 29:11).

Paul gives us some very interesting remarks about anger in Ephesians 4:26: "Be ye angry, and sin not: let not the sun go down upon your wrath." Paul is saying that it is okay to be emotionally moved. But the challenge however, is to not let it move into the wrath zone. Our hearts must be clear of all anger by sundown. You may be angry but don't let it cause you to sin. Anger must not become an obsession for the devil to use against us. Thus, God is not asking us to be stoic in the midst of wrong. He is only asking us to properly use our emotions.

Fifth, the Bible teaches that we can control our anger. This is not believed by some Christians. I have heard members of the church say, "I have tried but just can't control my temper." Let's notice again what the wise man said in the book of Proverbs: "A fool gives full vent to his anger, but a wise man keeps himself under control" (29:11). "Better a patient man than a warrior, a man who controls his temper than one who takes a city" (16:32). Paul wrote, "Get rid of bitterness, rage and anger, brawling and slander, along with every form of malice" (Ephesians 4:31). Surely, God wouldn't command us to do something if we couldn't do it! It has been rightly said that if Christianity hasn't done anything for your temper it hasn't done anything for you. You can be angry—but don't sin. With God's help we can control our anger. Tryon Edwards said, "To rule one's anger is well; to prevent it is still better." We must control our anger. Seneca said, "Anger, if not restrained, is frequently more hurtful to us than the injury that provokes it."

TIPS FOR CONTROLLING ANGER

1. In order to win over anger you must have a strong desire to do so. This is the beginning place. How strong is your desire?

2. Remember the tragic results of sinful and wrong anger. Dr. S. I. McMillen, in his book *None Of These Diseases*, makes the following statement: "However, fatal heart attacks can be triggered by 'anger in all degress, depress and anxiety,' according to Dr. Roy R. Grinker, one of the medical directors of Michael Reese Hospital in Chicago. This doctor states that anxiety places more stress on the heart than any other stimulus, including physical exercise and fatigue." (p. 60).

3. Remember you are not trying to free yourself from all anger. Some anger is healthy and needful. Not

all anger is sinful.

4. Practice James 1:19: ". . . let every man be swift to hear, slow to speak, slow to wrath."

5. Don't internalize your anger. This is like a pressure cooker: sooner or later the lid will blow off. Anger must be handled in a Biblical manner.

6. Prayerfully confront others who may be involved in your problem. This is not to blame them but to use them as part of the solution.

7. Ask yourself: "Why am I feeling angry?"; "Is there a valid basis for my anger?"; "What can I do to handle it?"; "What passage of Scripture is being violated?"

8. Never forget this truth: You can stop creating your anger any time you choose.

9. Remember that your anger won't change others; neither will it cause them to think better of you.

10. Rectify any wrongs that may exist between you and brethren. Read Matthew 5:23, 24; 18:15-17.

11. Remember God commands us not to let anger lead to sin (Ephesians 4:26).

12. Work on redirecting your anger. Let it lead you to solutions instead of bitterness and resentment.

13. Be aware of situations that cause you to lose control. It may be wise to avoid these situations in the early stages of your efforts to win over anger.

14. Ask your spouse or friend to help you with your anger control program. You may work out an

agreement where you will let it be known when you are beginning to lose your cool.

15. Be quick to forgive. Even if it requires seven time in one day (cf. Luke 17:1-5).

16. Remember that you can't control the actions and speech of others, but you can control how you react to them.

17. Replace your anger with love. Read I Corinthians 13.

18. Do something positive for the other person: "Therefore if thine enemy hunger, feed him; if he thirst, give him drink: for in so doing thou shalt heap coals of fire on his head" (Romans 12:20).

19. Don't associate with hot-tempered people: "Do not associate with a man given to anger; or go with a hot-tempered man, lest you learn his ways, and find a snare for yourself" (Proverbs 22:24, 25).

20. Use your creative imagination to win over anger. Rehearse in your mind the plan you will use to win over anger. See yourself winning in a situation that you normally get mad in. Also, meditate on the verses that teach us not to be angry.

21. Take a dose of your favorite exercise when you feel a spell of anger coming on.

22. Pray for help and wisdom from God (cf. James 1:2-5).

23. Stop pinning labels on people. When you think, for example, that a person is stupid or dumb, his actions will usually raise anger in you. Think of everyone as created in God's image.

24. Put in writing your plan for winning over anger. Do it now.

25. Thank God for irritations because they are growth opportunities (cf. Romans 8:28). Each victory makes you stronger in the Lord.

26. Put yourself in the other person's shoes. Try to see his point. Empathy is a great virtue.

CONCLUSION

Anger is an emotional capacity given to man by God. It plays a positive role in man's daily life. The challenge he is faced with, however, is to keep it under proper control. It is like a boomerang: it always comes back to you, sometimes with very serious consequences. The quest is, in Paul's words, to "Be angry, and sin not."

The child of God is called to a life of self-control. This means that he must have proper control over his temper. Someone wisely said, "Wise anger is like a fire from the flint; there is a great ado to bring it out; and when it does come, it is out again immediately." Paley wrote: "All anger is not sinful, because some degree of it, and on some occasions, is inevitable. But it becomes sinful and contradicts the rule of Scripture when it is conceived upon slight and inadequate provocation, and when it continues long."

"Anger," wrote the wise man, "resteth in the bosom of fools" (Ecclesiastes 7:9). His point is that no one gets hurt more than the person who becomes bitter and resentful as a result of uncontrolled anger. It is like the man who committed suicide to get even with his wife because she didn't appreciate him.

God's word guarantees that we can win over anger. The challenge is to begin our plan of action today. The next step is up to YOU!

FOR THOUGHT AND DISCUSSION

1. Why should we study anger?
2. When was the last time you were angry?
3. What is anger?
4. What role does thought play in creating anger?
5. Discuss the various forms of anger.
6. Can you think of additional forms of anger?
7. In what sense is anger good?
8. How does anger relate to God?
9. Give an example of uncontrolled anger in the Bible.
10. Discuss Jesus and anger.
11. Discuss Ephesians 4:26.
12. What suggestions do you have for winning over anger?
13. Should a person free himself from all anger?
14. How do you plan to use this lesson?
15. What additional thoughts or questions do you have?

CHAPTER TEN

WINNING OVER AN UNFORGIVING SPIRIT

"Generous and magnanimous minds are readiest to forgive; and it is a weakness and impotency of mind to be unable to forgive." (Lord Bacon)

INTRODUCTION

"What can Jesus Christ do for you now?" asked an inhuman slave-master, during the act of applying the lacerating whip to the already half-murdered slave. "Him," replied the slave, "teach me to forgive you, massa."

The world needs to be taught how to forgive. This is evident by the unforgiving spirit which abounds in our land, as well as in the hearts of many who profess to be Christians.

"I know what you say is right, and I understand what the Bible says about forgiveness, but he has hurt me too many times. I can't forgive him."

"I will forgive him but I assure you that I shall never forget it!"

"I won't forgive her until she proves herself. She has to earn my forgiveness."

These three quotations came from persons who were struggling with forgiveness. Their ranks are joined by thousands on a daily basis. Forgiveness is one of the hardest things for a person to do. It is difficult to win over an unforgiving spirit, especially if it has been held for many years. Children learn at an early age how to practice resentment and grudge bearing, which are qualities of an unforgiving spirit.

A person who can't forgive others breaks down the bridge over which he must pass himself; for every one, at one time or another, has need to be forgiven. As when the seaworm makes a hole in the shell of the mussel, the hole is filled with a pearl; likewise, when the human heart is pierced by an injury, forgiveness is like a pearl, healing and filling up the wound. Mark Twain wisely said, "Forgiveness is the fragrance the violet sheds on the heel that crushed it." An unforgiving spirit hurts the person who has it far more than the one he needs to forgive. This is why it is in man's best interest to practice forgiveness.

WHAT IS FORGIVENESS?

Forgiveness relates to some unfavorable action perpetrated against you that you no longer charge the perpetrator with. Forgiveness is an action of the mind. It can't do anything about what someone has done, but it can control how you respond to the wrong. Harboring it or letting it go takes place in the mind. Forgiveness is a choice to mark an end to consideration of a wrong or hurt. Unforgiveness is just the opposite: It holds resentment.

Forgiveness means to cancel, and the penalty is what we cancel. In a school in Ireland, one boy struck another; and, when he was about to be punished, the injured boy begged for his pardon. The school master asked, "Why do you wish to keep him from being whipped?" The boy replied, "I have read in the Bible that our Lord Jesus Christ said that we should forgive our enemies; and therefore I forgive him, and beg you not to punish him for my sake."

Forgiveness means to give up resentment and any desire for another to be punished. When Stephen was being stoned because of his faith in Jesus Christ, ". . . he kneeled down, and cried with a loud voice, Lord, lay not this sin to their charge. And when he had said this, he fell asleep" (Acts 7:60).

Human forgiveness, in a sense, is like Divine forgiveness. Jesus taught us to "forgive our debts, as we forgive our debtors" (Matthew 6:12). If certain conditions are fulfilled, Biblically speaking, there is no limitation to Christ's law of forgiveness. "Then came Peter to him, and said, Lord, how oft shall my brother sin against me, and I forgive him? till seven times? Jesus saith unto him, I say not unto thee, Until seven times: but, Until seventy times seven" (Matthew 18:21, 22).

Forgiveness is never cruel or ugly but is always rendered in a spirit of love and humility. Henry Ward Beecher left us these powerful words that describe the ugly attitude some approach forgiveness with: "There is an ugly kind of forgiveness in this world, – a kind of hedgehog forgiveness, shot out like quills. Men take one who has offended, and sit him down before the blowpipe of their indignation, and scorch him, and burn his fault into him; and, when they have kneaded him sufficiently with their fiery darts, then – they forgive him."

Forgiveness does not mean that I must also immediately forget. There is no such command in the Bible. Some persons believe that forgiveness is synonymous with forgetting. This is not true. Forgetting must be worked on after forgiveness occurs. Forgiveness is not a miraculous act that automatically erases your memory of an event in the past. In forgiving you have promised to never raise the issue again or hold the other person accountable. You will not dwell on the past action when it comes into your mind; rather, you will thank God for helping you to forgive the person. In time you will have longer and longer periods of not remembering the incident, as God helps you win over an unforgiving spirit.

In closing this section it is important for us to notice a few things that do not constitute forgiveness.

1. Forgiveness is not whitewash of sin or giving your stamp of approval to sin. An angry wife expressed it this way, "If I forgive Harold, he will think I am agreeing with his actions." Harold had repented of his sin, and God had forgiven him (cf. I John 1:8, 9). Surely the wife must know that God forgives, but in so doing, He doesn't agree with man's sin.

2. Forgiveness is not a condescension. Some people in forgiving demonstrate a spirit of superiority. They act as though they are better than you are; after all, you are the one who needs to be forgiven. This attitude is seen in such expressions as, "You've hurt me, but I'll be gracious and forgive you."

3. Forgiveness is not the cleansing of the person's record by an act of your justice. This is seen in the attitude that metes out a penalty to be served, after which forgiveness is granted. One lady told her husband, after he had admitted being unfaithful to her, "I will give you six months to prove yourself. If after six months every thing is okay, I will forgive you." How would you like for God to treat you like this lady treated her husband?

4. Forgiveness is not accumulated, delayed or suspended justice. A mother told her son, after he had broken a lamp, "I'll forgive you this time, but I'll tear your ear off next time!" Biblically, if there is a next time, and the mother truly forgave her son, she must not bring up the past broken lamp which she forgave him for breaking. This is how real forgiveness works.

Forgiveness, in summary, involves four basic facts: (1) The isolation of a wrong that you leave in the past; (2) the cancelling of any punishment or penalty you feel the act warrants; (3) the changing of your emotional response to the past event; and (4) working on forgetting it. When you forgive you promise to never bring it up again. Forgiveness, like *agape* love, has nothing to do with your feelings. It is a deliberate decision of your mind to cancel how you are responding to the actions of another. Many times I hear persons say, "I just don't feel like forgiving . . . should I do it when I don't feel like it? I don't want to be a hypocrite." You must forgive in spite of how you feel. After you forgive, God will help you bring your feelings in line with your decision to cancel the penalty. Forgiveness is commanded; it is not hypocritical to obey God's command. You must forget your feelings and forgive!

THE BIBLE AND FORGIVENESS

The capacity and possibility of forgiveness was given to man by God. In fact, God Himself sets the example in forgiving. The Psalmist wrote: "Lord, thou hast been favorable unto the land: . . . Thou hast forgiven the iniquity of the people, thou hast covered all their sin. Thou hast taken away all thy wrath: thou hast turned thyself from the fierceness of thine anger" (Psalm 85:1-3). When God forgives He cancels His anger and any penalty due man. When God forgives He blots out man's sin (cf. Isaiah 44:21, 22). When something is blotted out it is removed. It will never be brought up again. This is why David wrote, "Blessed is he whose transgression is forgiven, whose sin is covered" (Psalm 32:1).

The greatest example of forgiveness is the perfect Son of God asking the Father to forgive those who were crucifying Him: ". . . Father, forgive them; for they know not what they do . . ." (Luke 23:34). This model of forgiveness should always stay in our minds as a motivational force to help us forgive others.

Jesus made it very clear that our forgiveness depends upon our forgiving others: "And when you stand praying, forgive, if ye have ought against any: that your Father also which is in heaven may forgive your trespasses. But if ye do not forgive, neither will your Father which is in heaven forgive your trespasses" (Mark 11:25, 26).

The apostle Paul was a man who practiced forgiveness. He wrote: "To whom ye forgive any thing, I forgive also: for if I forgave any thing, to whom I forgave it, for your sakes forgave I it in the person of Christ; lest Satan should get an advantage of us: for we are not ignorant of his devices" (II Corinthians 2:11, 12). Paul's motivation to forgive came from Christ. He knew that Satan wanted him to have an unforgiving spirit. He resisted him.

Jesus taught that we should forgive others because we have been forgiven. In His parable of the Unmerciful Servant, He said, "Then his lord, after that he had called him, said unto him, O thou wicked servant, I forgave thee all that debt, because thou desiredst me: Shouldest not thou also have had compassion on thy fellowservant, even as I had pity on thee? And his lord was wroth, and delivered him to the tormentors, till he should pay all that was due unto him. So likewise shall my heavenly Father do also unto you, if ye from the hearts forgive not every one his brother their trespasses" (Matthew 18:32-35).

SEVEN TIMES IN ONE DAY

Admit it or not, nothing is more challenging for the Christian than to practice the virtue of forgiveness. Many upon discussing this subject, will readily admit that it is the most difficult command to obey. As we have seen, the commands to forgive are not arbitrary, as some seem to think, and as others are demonstrating by their actions and attitudes. Jesus made it clear that forgiveness is perpetual in nature. He said unto Peter, upon being asked how often one should forgive, ". . . I say not unto thee, until seven times: but, until seventy times seven" (Matthew 18:21, 22).

Forgiveness! What a challenge. While we properly understand that Jesus is not teaching a literal 490 times in forgiveness, we do, however, face the danger of practicing it on a too general, or too broad, basis. Jesus narrows it down for us to a DAILY practice. He said:

> "Take heed to yourself: if thy brother trespass against thee, rebuke him; and if he repent, forgive him. And if he trespass against thee seven times in a day, and seven times in a day turn again to thee, saying, I repent; thou shalt forgive him" (Luke 17: 3, 4). Yes you read it right! Jesus said SEVEN TIMES IN ONE DAY.

Many think they have fulfilled their responsibility if they forgive a person one time, not in one day, but once in a lifetime. Practicing forgiveness on an unlimited basis, which is what Jesus is teaching, would correct many of the problems in the home, in the church, on the job, in personal matters, etc. In the final analysis, we have no choice in the matter, if we want to be pleasing unto God.

How should you act after you have forgiven someone? Forgiveness is more than the cancelling of a penalty. It should mean the restoration of a broken fellowship; the kind that occurs when God forgives us. Some persons claim to forgive and continue to treat the supposed forgiven person as an enemy. Forgiving seven times in one day also means accepting back into fellowship seven times. This is the real power of forgiveness.

A Christian will find it cheaper to forgive than to resent. Forgiveness saves one from anger, hatred, unhappiness, and an unforgiving spirit. It was Pope who said, "To err is human; to forgive, divine." Can you forgive seven times in one day?

KEYS TO FORGIVENESS

First, there are no shortcuts to forgiveness. Either you forgive or you don't. A man by the name of Lord Herbert wrote, "Forgiveness is the most necessary and proper work of every man; for, though, when I do not a just thing, or a charitable, or a wise, another man may do it for me, yet no man can forgive my enemy but myself."

Second, forgiveness must take place NOW. Tomorrow may be too late. It is reported that before the death of Frederick the Great, he was told that he should forgive his enemies. "Dorothy," he said to the queen, "write to your brother that I forgive him of all the evil he has done to me; but wait till I am dead first."

Third, forgiveness does not involve immediate forgetting. We must not wait until time has worn away a wrong before we forgive. We forgive and the matter is once and for all left in the past. Forgetfulness will come in time, but only after forgiveness. An old preacher put it this way, "Forgive and forget. When you bury a mad dog, don't leave his tail above the ground." Forgiveness does not leave the hatchet handle sticking out of the ground.

Fourth, forgiving makes you a winner in God's sight. "He who has mastered the grace of forgiveness is far more triumphant than he who has managed to see that no wrong to him is gone unavenged," wrote Lloyd M. Mattson.

Fifth, always remember the forgiveness you have received from God. Can you do less than forgive others after you have been forgiven of so much?

Sixth, be careful to examine why you may be having difficulty in forgiving a person. Why is the offense so difficult to forgive? Have you discussed it with the person?

Seventh, use your imagination to develop a plan for forgetting after you have forgiven. Imagine yourself acting in a favorable way with the person you have forgiven. See yourself as making friends with the person.

Eighth, thank God for helping you practice forgiveness. It is through His design and by His power that it is possible.

Ninth, be careful to be honest with your feelings after you forgive. Do you still think about the wrong? How do you treat the person who has been forgiven? Do you have love for the person (*agape*)? If you have forgiven your mind must not remain in turmoil. Remember the pretense of forgiveness is an obstacle to real forgiveness.

Tenth, renew your mind daily. This will involve a daily meditation on God's word. Each day cast out any negative thoughts that enter your mind relative to forgiveness. Your challenge is to never bring it up again once you have forgiven.

CONCLUSION

When the books of a certain Scotch doctor were examined after his death, it was found that a number of accounts were crossed out with a note: "Forgiven–too poor to pay." But the physician's wife decided that these accounts must be paid, and proceeded to sue for the money. The judge asked one question: "Is this your husband's handwriting?" When she replied that it was, he said, "Then there is no court in the land that can obtain this money when he has written the word 'Forgiven'."

When God forgives our sins, it is not possible for Him to bring them back up and use them against us. Notice very carefully His promises: "Behold, the days come, saith the Lord, that I will make a new covenant with the house of Israel . . . for I will forgive their iniquity, and I will remember their sin no more" (Jeremiah 31:31, 34). "As far as the east is from the west, so far hath he removed our transgressions from us" (Psalm 103:12).

"Mother," said a dying girl, "please get the Bible and read to me that passage about the blood which cleanseth from sin. I fear some of my sins are too great to be forgiven. Look whether it says, 'all sin,' for I do not remember." "Yes," replied her mother, "these are the exact words, 'The blood of Jesus Christ His Son cleanseth us from all sin'." "Oh, how sweet!" said the girl whose life was almost gone.

There is no sweeter word than FORGIVENESS. It describes what the blood of Christ has done for us (cf. Matthew 26:28; Acts 20:28; Revelation 1:5). It is the incentive for us to go and do likewise. Is there anyone you need to forgive? DO IT NOW!

FOR THOUGHT AND DISCUSSION

1. Why is forgiveness important in daily living?
2. Is it easy for most people to forgive? How about you?
3. Define forgiveness.
4. Give an illustration of how forgiveness works.
5. What is "divine forgiveness"?
6. How does forgiveness relate to forgetting?
7. Discuss the four basic facts about forgiveness.
8. Discuss the forgiveness of Christ.
9. What will happen if we don't forgive?
10. What motivated Paul to forgive?
11. Why is forgiveness so difficult for some persons?
12. Discuss Luke 17:3, 4.
13. If a person doesn't ask you for forgiveness, do you have to forgive him?
14. How should you act after you have forgiven someone?
15. How do you plan to use this lesson in your life?

CHAPTER ELEVEN

WINNING OVER STRESS

"I will lie down and sleep in peace, for you alone, O Lord, make me dwell in safety" (Psalm 4:8).

INTRODUCTION

There is a major enemy stalking our land. It is not a respecter of persons. It seeks to devour the peace and happiness of everyone it touches if not properly controlled. *Each year:*

* It causes billions of dollars to be lost in wages to workers.
* It is a major contributor to heart attacks.
* It plays a significant role in raising the blood pressure of millions of Americans.
* It is suspected as a cause of cancer.
* It leads to alcohol and drug abuse.
* It produces sleepless nights.
* It causes problems in the home. It contributes to divorce.
* It leads to depression and anxiety.
* It contributes to decisions to commit suicide.
* It causes fatigue, headaches, backaches, allergies, nervousness, tiredness, dizziness, and a host of other symptoms.
* It drains energy from the body and mind.
* It kills many of its victims.

What is it? *Stress*!

Richard's weekly routine consisted of some of the following things:

1. He worked 40 hours in a factory.

2. He got up at four each morning to deliver papers before he went to work.

3. He spent a minimum of two hours each day fighting the freeway traffic going to and from work.

4. On Saturdays he was taking a course in welding and blueprint reading at a local vocational technical school.

5. He stayed up late on Saturday nights preparing for his Bible class the next morning at church.

6. Sundays after lunch, he visited the hospitals and convalescent homes; then back to church Sunday night.

Everyone was surprised when Richard, at age 35, had a heart attack. Stress was identified as one of the major causes of his attack. He was living life in the fast lane; his body couldn't properly handle all the stress placed upon it. Another victim of burnout bites the dust.

Each day thousands like Richard hit the streets in America promising themselves that today will be different. Today they are going to slow down; there will be less tension, no frustration or flurry. Instead, they step into a world that once again challenges them to shift their pace into high gear. The deadlines, rushing traffic, appointments, problems, noise, racing clock, and a host of other things tighten their neck and back muscles. They become uptight and irritable. One more ounce of pressure will cause them to blow their control valve. That ounce of pressure may be provided by the wife or children, or some other person, as the victim of too much stress drags himself/herself home.

Stress does not strike all individuals equally. In their book entitled *Stress*, Walter McQuade and Ann

Aikman, make this observation on this point: "Some people seem to thrive on it (stress, etc.); it is their meat—Churchill comes to mind. A rather different example is the Russian writer Alexander Solzhenitsyn. If you spend your life doing something that really matters to you, and doing it well, you can withstand a great deal.

"Most of us do not fare so well. For airport flight dispatchers stress is endemic. Assembly-line mechanics, waitresses, taxi drivers, college students competing to get into medical school—all are but anything but immune. People living in a rapidly deteriorating neighborhood know stress well. Even youthful residents of a rural commune, as winter progresses, the larder shrinks, and communal tempers become edgy, may find themselves susceptible. All social shifts generate stress, and there are signs that women's vulnerability is increasing as fast as their independence. A century ago peptic ulcers were a woman's ailment, by a ratio of seven to three. Then, as frontier rigors were replaced by industrial ones, life got easier for women and harder for men, and from 1920 to 1940 nine out of ten victims were male. But since mid-century the incidence of ulcers in women is again on the rise." (pp. 6, 7, Bantam Books, N. Y., N. Y., 1974).

Stress out of control is dangerous for the Christian. This is why he must learn how to win over it.

WHAT IS STRESS?

Webster gives us the following definitions of stress: 1. "strain; pressure; esp., force exerted upon the body that tends to strain or deform its shape. 2. urgency; importance. 3. tension; strained exertion: as, the stress of war . . ."

According to Dr. Hans Selye, the father of modern stress research, stress is the result of demands made upon the body. In his book *The Stress of Life*, he defines stress as: "The nonspecific response of the body to any demand."

In a paper called *For Your Good Health*, which is distributed by the Martin Luther Hospital Medical Center,

Aneheim, California, and dated summer, 1982, we have a description of stress: "We use the word *stress* to describe our reactions when events or experiences cause mental tension or when our bodies strain to function normally. Stress is reflected as accelerated heartbeat, a rise in blood pressure, bowel or urinary changes, headache or other localized pain, cramped muscles or skin eruptions. It can also affect one's ability to think or behave rationally or appropriately.

"When mental or emotional stress results in changes in the body's normal physiological pattern or functions, the condition is frequently described as *psychosomatic* in origin (*psyche*: mind; *soma*: body)."

In simple terms stress is the wear and tear of life. It is not possible to avoid all stress entirely. In fact, some stress is good for us. The key, however, is in how we adjust to it, and in its duration. It is the long term stress that may kill us. The damage comes when the adrenal flow is too long. Man must have proper relief from stress.

It is impossible to live without stress. In fact, stress keeps life interesting. Every activity we engage in produces some form of stress. Each session of physical exercise involves stress. Through a gradual increase of stress fitness occurs. When we think and exercise our minds stress occurs. The challenge, however, is to balance stress in our daily lives. Prolonged stress can create disease and emotional problems. Short-term stress is a normal function which is normally handled by the glands and organs without any problem. To function comfortably we must recognize stress and our capacity to handle it.

Stress has many faces. Dr. Kurt W. Donsbach, in his booklet entitled *Stress*, has this to say: "Stress comes in many different forms. We are all too familiar with what can be called emotional stress and the resultant nervous reactions that can occur. But stress may also be mechanical, physical, nutritional, chemical, as well as the result of radiation. In essence, stress can be considered anything that tends to change the control that one would ordinarily have over their body and/or emotions." (p. 5)

STRESS ACCUMULATION

The damage stress may cause seems to be determined by two factors: (1) the kind of stress, and (2) the frequency of the stress. Repeated severe stress makes it difficult for a person to escape emotional or physical problems as a result of it.

Drs. Thomas H. Holmes and Richard Rahe, of the University of Washington School of Medicine, have developed "The Social Readjustment Rating Scale." They believe that the rate of change in a person's life is related to a probability of change in his health. A person can only adjust to a certain number of changes without it affecting his health. Holmes and Rahe assign a numerical value to a list of 43 life events which are stressful in a person's life. Death is rated 100 life-change units and is listed first on the scale. A minor violation of the law is rated 11 life-change units and is listed last on the scale. They conclude that a person through his own strength can't handle 300 or more units in a twelve-month period without experiencing some physical or emotional problem during the two years that follow the accumulation of the 300 points.

The reality of life reminds us that changes in life rarely occur in isolation. They are like dominos stacked in a row. When you push one it moves the others. Using the Holmes and Rahe scale let's notice how a family move (rated 20) may usually entail these changes too: change in working conditions (25), change in social activities (18), change in church activities (19), mortgage over $10,000 (31), change to different line of work (36), change in financial state (38), change in number of family get-togethers (15). Thus in a matter of days because of a move (to another state) a person may accumulate 222 Life Change Units. This doesn't take into account other problems that may surround the change (move). Even though some changes may be good, Holmes and Rahe indicate in their research that too much change in a short period may take its toll on the body's ability to adapt and cope.

Dr. Hans Selye, in his book *The Stress of Life*, lists 31 stress danger signs which are easy to detect. Selye believes when a person is under stress he tends to produce a symptom in some part of his body. From Selye's list I have selected the following and his corresponding number to give you an idea of the kinds of symptoms he is talking about: (1) General irritability, hyperexcitation, or depression; (4) Impulsive behavior, emotional instability; (10) Emotional tension and alertness, feelings of being "keyed up"; (19) The frequent need to urinate; (23) pain in the neck and lower back; (31) proneness to accidents.

In closing this section the words of Selye should serve as our guideline for using any of the stress indicators, scales or tests: "It is our ability to cope with the demands made by the events in our lives, not the quality or intensity of the events, that counts."

The hope of the Christian is in God and His word. Through Christ Jesus we are more than conquerors, and have resources for coping with stress.

Any Moment

"Any moment of hating,
Any moment of lying,
Any moment of resentment,
Is a moment of dying.
Any moment of loving,
Any moment of giving,
Any moment of thankfulness,
Is a moment of living.
All our moments add together
Like the digits in a sum
And the answer tells us plain
Whether life or death shall come."

–Martin Cecil

The words in "Any Moment" are about stress and its

affect on our lives. It reminds us in simple poetic form that too much stress is not good for us.

THE BIBLE AND STRESS

There are many examples of stress in the Bible. A study of some of these will help us see that rarely is a person exempt from pressure.

Moses is our first example of a man being in a stressful situation. In Exodus chapter 18 we read the account of this great leader trying to provide guidance for the nation of Israel. It was more than one man could do. Finally his father-in-law, Jethro, arrives on the scene and gives him some wise advice relative to his work with the people. Jethro asks: "What is this thing that thou doest to the people? why sittest thou thyself alone, and all the people stand by thee from morning unto evening . . . The thing that thou doest is not good. Thou wilt surely wear away, both thou, and this people . . ." (Exodus 18:14, 17, 18). The solution to Moses' problem was to select helpers from among the people (Exodus 18:21-24). Through their help he would relieve himself and the people from a stressful situation. Thus, Moses learned a lesson that most people never learn: You can't burn the candle at both ends without getting trapped in the middle.

David is another example of a person experiencing a great variety of stressful situations. His life was full of pressure, beginning with the challenge of Goliath and continuing through his reign as King. Some especially stressful events were:

1. When he was running from Saul in an effort to save his life (I Samuel 21-27). It was during this time that he wrote the Twenty-third Psalm. This Psalm has provided more help for people during times of stress than perhaps any other set of words in the Bible.

2. David lamented over Saul and Jonathan (II Samuel 1:19-27).

3. His great sin with Bathsheba (II Samuel 11:1 - 12:24).

4. The plot to murder Uriah must have been stressful.

5. His mourning over the death of Absalom (II Samuel 18:1-33).

A third example of stress is the man James uses as the champion of patience, Job. It is interesting to note that an article appearing in the July 3, 1981, Volume 246, No. 1 issue of the *Journal of the American Medical Association*, had this to say about Job's stress: "Physicians caring for crisis-ridden families have often searched world literature for guidance and wisdom. Outstanding is the story of Job with its three major themes: (1) the impact of concurrent cataclysmic events on one man, including a wracking illness . . .; (2) the advice of well-meaning friends who do more harm than good; and (3) the inquiring but unrelenting faith of Job." (page 60, by George Rainsford, M. D., and Stanley Schuman, M. D., D. P. H.).

One has but to read the book of Job to see the great stress this man of God was under. Some of the major components of his stress are as follows:

1. Job was tried by the loss of all his wealth (Job 1:13-17).

2. Job lost his ten children at one time (Job 1:18, 19). This alone would be 1000 units on the life-change scale.

3. Job was tried by the devices of Satan (Job 2:6).

4. Job was tried by the loss of his physical health (Job 2:7-9, etc.).

5. Job was rejected by his friends. He was lonely (Job 2:11ff).

6. Job was mentally distressed (Job 3:1ff).

7. Job was tried by the conduct of his wife (Job 2:9).

8. Job was in a constant state of frustration because he couldn't get his questions answered.

Through all his stress, Job trusted God and patiently waited for vendication. In the end his victory came (Job 42:10-17). Patience is a great balm for stress.

The Lord Jesus Christ is our best example of stress and how to properly handle it. The prophet Isaiah foretold of some of His sorrows: "He is despised and rejected of men; a man of sorrows, and acquainted with grief . . . stricken, smitten of God, and afflicted" (Isaiah 53:3, 4).

We also learn from the example of Christ that no matter how good a person is, he can't escape the pressures of life. Stress comes to everyone.

From the beginning of His public ministry until His death on the cross, Christ was in one stressful situation after another. In every case He was in control of Himself. Some examples of stressful situations He was in are as follows:

1. His own people (Jews) rejected Him (John 1:11).

2. He was pressed by crowds (Mark 4:1, 2).

3. People tried to trap Him with questions (Luke 10:25).

4. The Jews misunderstood Him (John 7:10-13).

5. They sought to kill Him (John 5:16).

6. They called Him names (Matthew 11:19).

7. He must have been frustrated at times with the disciples (Mark 4:38-41).

8. People were constantly asking Him to do something for them (John 6:15-21).

9. He was arrested and kept up all night in a mock trial (Mark 14:35 - 15:15).

10. The beating and suffering before His death on the cross (Mark 15:19-35).

The Prince of Peace was the master of handling stress and the pressures of life. He invites us to yoke up with Him so that He can help us win over stress (Matthew 11:28-30).

Our final example of stress is the man who went from being the persecutor to being persecuted, Saul of Tarsus, who later became the Apostle Paul. A number of times in his writings he shares with us some of the pressure points in his life as a Christian.

1. He had a burden for the salvation of his countrymen (Romans 10:1-4).

2. He was persecuted, but not forsaken; cast down, but not destroyed (II Corinthians 4:9).

3. He was troubled on every side, but not distressed (II Corinthians 4:8).

4. He was often beaten and imprisoned (II Corinthians 11:23).

5. He was beaten with rods, stoned, and shipwrecked (II Corinthians 11:25).

6. He was in danger many times as he traveled to preach the gospel (II Corinthians 11:26).

7. He was weary, in pain, cautious, hungry, thirsty, and often without proper clothing (II Corinthians 11:27).

8. He had a daily anxiety for all the churches (II Corinthians 11:28).

How could one man endure so many life-changes? The answer is CHRIST. Paul believed he could do all things through his Lord (Philippians 4:13); and that Christ was the source of power (Ephesians 3:20) for winning. This suffering saint had learned the fine art of being content in every situation (Philippians 4:11). He had inner control regardless of the outer pressure.

KEYS TO WINNING OVER STRESS

First, remember that we create tension by our inner response to our environment. Thus, we are in control of how much stress we let affect us.

Second, remember that a certain amount of stress is normal. It is the amount and frequency that is critical, as well as how you handle it. The body has certain built-in responses to stress.

Third, watch for signs and symptoms of stress, and examine the causes. Take control of your life by realizing your stress level.

Fourth, be sure that you have made peace with God. We are promised all spiritual blessing through Christ (cf. Ephesians 1:3). One of these blessings is peace. Jesus said, "Peace I leave with you, my peace I give unto you: not as the world giveth, give I unto you . . . These things I have spoken unto you, that ye might have peace. In the world ye shall have tribulation: be ye of good cheer; I have overcome the world" (John 14:27; 16:33). Peter wrote, "Casting all your care upon him; for he careth for you" (I Peter 5:7). Peace is a great remedy for stress.

Fifth, in order to win over stress a person must learn to relax. Jesus, in the midst of his busy activities, said, ". . . come ye yourself apart in to a desert place, and rest a while: for they were many coming and going, and they had no leisure so much as to eat" (Mark 6:31). Tim

Hansel, in his book *When I Relax I Feel Guilty*, gives us some good remarks on real leisure. He writes: "Leisure is more than just nonwork. It is a point of contact with reality and a catalyst for new experiences, new ideas, new people, and new places. It is the time when the gift of wholeness again becomes a hope and possibility.

"In order for this to happen, three things must be done. First, we must be convinced of the importance of quality leisure in our lives – not superficial play . . . Second, we must understand how to practice quality leisure. We cannot assume it will just happen. It doesn't. Third, we must then act on what we know to be true. This is both the difficult part and the most exciting" (p. 31, David C. Cook Publishing Co., copyright 1979). Even God rested on the seventh day. Jehovah said, "Be still and know that I am God . . ." (Isaiah 46:10).

Sixth, exercise is another great way to relieve some of the daily stresses in life. It also helps us bear up under stress in general. As the blood starts rushing and the muscles start expanding and stretching, the knots start dissolving.

Seventh, daily periods of meditation on God's word is a powerful medicine for stress. The Psalmist wrote, "O how love I thy law! It is my meditation all the day . . . Trouble and anguish have taken hold on me: yet thy commandments are my delights" (Psalm 119:97, 143).

Eighth, examine your schedule and remove the items that aren't important. Most people are under stress because they have too much to do. Learn to say no. Walk away from a job temporarily. Choose your goals very carefully and don't pressure yourself too much to achieve them.

Ninth, use your creative imagination during periods of relaxation. Set aside a period each day and deeply relax all your muscles. Practicing breathing slowly and deeply. In this state of relaxation imagine all of the stress draining out of your body.

Tenth, try to cut down on excessive noise. It can

play havoc on your nerves. Teach your teenagers how to use the volume controls on TV, the radio, and the stereo.

Eleventh, try to provide your body with a balanced diet. Such things as sugar and caffine can cause stress. Also, be careful about crash diets.

Twelfth, try not to be a perfectionist. "Do your best and forget about the rest" is a good motto for stress management. Be careful about self-created demands.

Thirteenth, proper time management is a positive way to eliminate stress. Don't become a slave to the clock. Do, however, learn and use some basic tools for time management. Your life will run smoother.

Fourteenth, arrange to have variety in your life. "All work and no play makes Jack's life a dull day." Escape and diversion are essential to stress management.

Fifteenth, if the problem of stress doesn't go away with various self-help approaches, you may want to see your physician for an examination.

CONCLUSION

Every day we are confronted with reminders of our stress filled society. There are TV specials; newspaper and magazine articles; lectures; seminars, etc., offering advice and help for persons suffering from stress. The vitamin manufacturers have even come up with special formulas to help us cope with stress. I have recently noticed such names as "Stresstabs," "Maxi-Stress," "Mega Stress," on vitamin bottles.

Stress is an individual thing; no two persons react the same way to the pressures and tensions of life. This is why it is difficult to give a sure-fire list of suggestions for handling stress. The key is knowledge of self, and then adapting self-help principles to your needs. It is up to you to learn stress-reduction techniques that will work for you.

Jesus Christ is the answer to all our needs. He not only sets us free from sin and guilt, He also gives us peace and joy. As we yoke up with Him our burdens become manageable. Peace is ours to possess; the challenge is to claim it. As we yield our lives to Him, He also sets us free from the consequences of the pressures of life (cf. John 8:32, 36).

Slow Me Down, Lord

By: Orin L. Crain

Slow me down, Lord.

Ease the pounding of my heart by the
quieting of my mind.

Steady my hurried pace with a vision
of the eternal reach of time.

Give me, amid the confusion of the day,
the calmness of the everlasting hills.

Break the tensions of my nerves and
muscles with soothing music of the
singing streams that live in my memory.

Teach me the art of taking minute
vacations–of slowing down to look at a
flower, to chat with a friend, to pat a dog,
to smile at a child, to read a few lines
from a good book.

Slow me down, Lord, and inspire me to
send my roots deep into the soil of life's
enduring values, that I may grow toward
my greater destiny.

Remind me each day that the race is not
always to the swift; that there is more to
life than increasing its speed.

Let me look upward to the towering oak
and know that it grew great and strong
because it grew slowly and well."

FOR THOUGHT AND DISCUSSION

1. Why is stress an enemy?
2. Do you believe that you successfully cope with stress?
3. Share an account of a person you know who suffered from stress.
4. Why do some people thrive on stress and others "break"?
5. Discuss some occupations that are stress producing.
6. Define stress.
7. How does stress affect your body? How do you feel?
8. Can a person live without any stress?
9. How does stress relate to emotions?
10. Discuss stress accumulation.
11. Have you seen the Holmes and Rahe life-change unit scale? Try to get a copy.
12. What are some of the major signs of stress?
13. Discuss Biblical examples of stress.
14. How do you plan to use this lesson?
15. Discuss the keys to handling stress.

CHAPTER TWELVE

WINNING OVER DEPRESSION

"Have courage for the great sorrows of life and patience for the small ones; and when you have laboriously accomplished your daily task, go to sleep in peace. God is awake." – Victor Hugo

INTRODUCTION

Three weeks ago I was shocked when I came upon this headline in my morning newspaper: *Depressed student, 10, kills himself*. The story related how the boy had taken the family gun and shot himself. Upon investigating the boy's conduct prior to his death, it was concluded that he was depressed and this was the cause of his action. How could a 10-year-old get that depressed? What has gone wrong with our society and homes that is producing such severe cases of depression? I don't have a final answer to these questions. I do know, however, that depression is a major health enemy in our nation.

In his book entitled *A New Beginning*, Gary Emery, Ph.D., in answering a question concerning what he has learned about depression, makes this sobering remark: "First, depression is a serious emotional disorder and a significant health problem. Suicide, a byproduct of depression, is a leading cause of death. Researchers now estimate that one out of seven people with severe depression will commit suicide. Up to forty thousand people do so every year; nearly all are depressed.

"Depression is not an isolated problem. Worldwide, over 100 million people are depressed. In your lifetime you run more than twenty percent risk of having a major or minor depression. And if you are a woman, the odds are higher, for depression strikes many more women than men."

Raymond had been without work for two months. His bills were going unpaid; his unemployment check was barely enough to provide food for his family. He had searched in vain for a job. He was becoming more and more of a recluse; his personal grooming was neglected, and he had lost his appetite. He would sit and stare at the walls for hours. In his rare conversations he would talk about how life wasn't worth living. Through encouragement and insistance from his wifc, hc finally agreed to see a counselor. It didn't take the counselor too long to diagnose Raymond's problem as depression. Thankfully, with God's help, as well as the counselor's help, Raymond was able to work through his depression and get a new lease on life.

Depression is no respecter of persons. He strikes the rich and poor, the educated and uneducated. I have seen religious leaders with it, as well as nonreligious persons with it. Depression doesn't depend upon what you have or your circumstances in life. It comes from within.

The AMA once suggested that more suffering comes from depression than any other single disease affecting man. Since this is true, and since it is also true that many Christians are suffering from depression, it becomes essential for us to learn how to win over depression.

WHAT IS DEPRESSION?

Depression is not a modern problem. It is the oldest known psychiatric illness. It was described by the ancient Greeks, who listed many of the same symptoms that still are being recognized by psychiatrists in our day. Hippocrates, the father of medicine, in his writings described man as having four temperaments. The one called "melancholia" was said to be produced by black, heavy blood circulating through the veins of the patient. This was a false observation.

What is depression? The *Dictionary of Psychology*,

page 30, defines depression as, "Melancholia, gloom, dejection." *The Psychology of Counseling*, by Clyde M. Narramore, defines depression as, "Undue sadness, dejection or melancholy. Feelings of worthlessness and guilt and often, apprehension. Stems primarily from inner emotional causes." (page 278).

Depression is a great mimic. In *Feeling Good*, Dr. David D. Burns has this to say: "Depression can mimic a great number of medical disorders because your mood swings often create a wide variety of puzzling physical symptoms. These include, to name a few, constipation, diarrhea, pain, insomnia or the tendency to sleep too much, fatigue, loss of sexual interest, light-headedness, trembling, and numbness." (page 35).

Depression is basically defined by the various symptoms a person has: What he feels, what he does, how he thinks. This is why it is essential for a person to be able to recognize some of the symptoms of depression. According to the Research Diagnostic Criteria (RDC), a clinical interview proceedure used in most depression research centers, you would be considered depressed if you answer yes to these two broad questions: *One*, have you had a distinct period of feeling down and unhappy or a distinct period of overall loss of pleasure and interest? And *two*, have you suffered from five of the following eight symptoms for at least two weeks: (1) appetite or weight change, (2) sleep problems, (3) excessive tiredness, (4) physically slowed down or agitated, (5) loss of interest or pleasure in usual activities, (6) feeling guilty, (7) slow thinking or indecisiveness, (8) thoughts of killing yourself.

Your susceptibility to depression is likely to depend on your age and sex. University of California investigators made a study of a representative sample of more than 1,000 adults from a metropolitan area, in which each person was interviewed four times over a 12-month period. The researchers found that females were twice as likely to be depressed (24 percent) as males. By age, persons 18 to 24 reported the highest rate of depression (27 percent). Those 45 to 64 reported the lowest (16 percent).

Depression has a direct effect upon your self-esteem. It effects what you think about yourself as a person as well as how you rate yourself. Unresolved depression causes a person to emphasize his bad traits and minimize his good ones. It's back to the truth that keeps reoccurring in this series of studies: How you evaluate your thoughts about yourself and your experiences determines your emotional reactions. A person who views the world in a distorted way must correct these distortions before he can win over depression.

Depression is not a sin. It is merely a signal that something is wrong in your life. If it is not properly handled, it could lead a person into sin. It is hard to think right and do right when your emotions are thrown off balance by the weight of depression. This is why we invite God to help us win over depression.

BIBLE EXAMPLES OF DEPRESSION

From our study of what depression is, we have no difficulty in realizing that many persons in the Bible were challenged by this emotion. I want to share a brief sketch of several Bible characters who seem to demonstrate moments of depression in their lives.

The first case I want to share is Moses. The account is recorded in Numbers 11. This great man of God had served as the leader of Israel through many challenging situations. He had confronted Pharoah on their belief; he led them across the Red Sea; he wanted to lead them to the promised land. But Moses became discouraged because of the murmuring of the people. Israel wanted flesh to eat instead of the manna God was providing (cf. Numbers 11:1-9).

Moses became so discouraged that the signs of depression became obvious in his conduct. He preferred to die than continue in the situation. Moses said, "I am not able to bear all this people alone, because it is too heavy for me. And if thou deal thus with me, kill me, I pray thee, out of hand, if I have found favor in thy sight; and let me not see my wretchedness (Numbers 11:14, 15).

God intervened and helped Moses. He gave Moses seventy men to help him bear his responsibility (Numbers 11:16-30). Jehovah also gave Israel flesh to eat (Numbers 11:17-23). Turning to God and trusting Him is the key to winning over depression. Also, getting help is good relief for depression.

King Saul had it all going for him until he rebelled against God (cf. I Samuel 15:8-35). Because of his actions he was rejected by God from reigning over Israel (I Samuel 16:1). As a result, "the spirit of the Lord departed from Saul, and an evil spirit from God troubled (i.e., terrified) him" (I Samuel 16:14).

Saul was told by a servant that music would be good therapy for his depression (16:16); the King consented and called for a musician (16:17). ". . . David took an harp, and played with his hand: so Saul was refreshed, and was well, and the evil spirit departed from him" (16:23).

It has been medically proven that certain kinds of music is good mood therapy.

Elijah, the great prophet of God, is another man who became so depressed that he desired death. The account is recorded in I Kings 19. The wicked queen Jezebel had threatened Elijah's life (19:2). After a day of running and not eating the prophet became negative: "But he himself went days journey into the wilderness, and came and sat down under a juniper tree: and he requested for himself that he might die; and said, It is enough; now, O Lord, take away my life; for I am no better than my fathers" (19:5).

Tired and frustrated the man of God fell asleep. God awoke the prophet through an angel who said to him, "Arise and eat" (19:5). The tired, weak and discouraged prophet was told to eat a second time (19:7) by the angel. The sustenance from the two meals was such that Elijah was able to live forty days in the wilderness of the strength it provided (19:8). Elijah, however, was still afraid and depressed (19:13, 14).

God told the prophet to get busy. There was work that he must do (19:15). He was to anoint Hazael to be king over Syria, and Jehu to be anointed king over Israel, and Elisha was to be anointed to be prophet in Elijah's place.

God also helped Elijah by telling him that he was not alone. There were 7,000 who had not bowed the knee to Baal (19:18). Elijah was reminded that things weren't as bad as they seemed. Through God's help victory came to Elijah. God is still helping his servants.

Our fourth example is Jonah, the prophet God called to go and preach repentance to Ninevah. Ninevah was the capital of Assyria. The Assyrians were enemies of Israel. God wanted the great city to be given a chance to repent and, thus, avoid destruction. Jonah, however, thought God should destroy the city.

Most Bible students are familiar with Jonah's attempt to run away from his assignment (Jonah 1). After a three day stay in the stomach of the great fish, he decided to obey God (Jonah 2).

Jonah goes through the city preaching repentance (Jonah 3:4-10), and the people obey his message. Thus, God spares them from destruction. This is too much for Jonah. He became very angry (4:1). Just as two other prophets had done, Jonah requests that God take his life from him (4:3). The depressed prophet goes and makes a booth to sulk under (4:4, 5). God caused a gourd to spring up and shadow Jonah's head, "to deliver him from grief. So Jonah was exceeding glad of the gourd" (4:6).

"And it came to pass, when the sun did arise, that God prepared a vehement east wind; and the sun beat upon the head of Jonah, that he fainted, and wished himself to die, and said, It is better for me to die than to live. And God said to Jonah, Doest thou well to be angry for the gourd? And he said, I do well to be angry, even unto death.

Then said the Lord, Thou hast had pity on the gourd, for the which thou hast not laboured, neither madest it grow; which came up in a night, and perished in a night" (Jonah 4:9-10).

We leave Jonah in an apparent state of depression. Some people find it difficult to accept God's counsel.

Judas is our fifth example of depression. As we see in chapter twenty-seven of Matthew, Judas' guilt led him into a state of deep depression. His guilt and subsequent suicide is the end result of unresolved depression.

"The Judas, which had betrayed him, when he saw that he was condemned, repented himself, and brought again the thirty pieces of silver to the chief priests and elders, Saying, I have sinned in that I have betrayed the innocent blood. And they said, What is that to us? see thou to that. And he cast down the pieces of silver in the temple, and departed, and went and hanged himself" (Matthew 27:3-5).

Depression is not the exclusive territory of the spiritually weak. The pages of God's word reveal that it was a frequent experience of many great leaders. We learn from their lives that God will help us if we will trust and serve Him.

SOME CAUSES OF DEPRESSION

Depression, like so many other emotional problems, arises from a variety of causes. What causes one person to become depressed may not cause another person to become depressed. There are, however, some basic causes of depression, that at various times, may be prevalent in the life of a depressed person. One or more of the following things may produce depression.

1. Negative thinking that produces a negative attitude toward life.

2. A failure to eat properly, as well as poor sleeping

habits will produce a tired body. A tired body is more prone to depression than a rested one.

3. Many times a certain medication a person is taking may cause depression. A person should check with his physician if he suspects it is causing his bouts with depression.

4. Physical illnesses or malfunctions may cause depression. For example studies show that the prevalence of depression-related problems is as high as 37 percent in hypertensive patients, compared to 4 to 12 percent in the general population.

5. A hormone deficiency or imbalance may contribute to depression. An example is a thyroid problem (e.g., secreting too much or not enough thyroxine).

6. Inflammation of the liver, called hepatitis, may contribute to depression.

7. Reactive grief may produce depression. The loss of a friend, relative, job, etc., may spark bouts of depression.

8. Unresolved emotional conflicts such as anger, guilt, low self-esteem, bitterness, unforgiveness, fear, anxiety, etc., contribute to depression.

9. When a person's life is not right with God there is a high chance that he will experience depression.

10. Rejection and loss of love is a major cause of depression. This ranks as one of the most devastating causes of depression in our society.

11. Discouragement and disappointment are at the top of the list of depression causes.

12. A lack of faith and trust in God and His word produce consequences that lead to depression. We must know God and His will for our lives before we can have true happiness and peace of mind.

13. Depression can be triggered by setting unrealistic goals for your life, as well as unattainable ones.

14. As strange as it may sound, temporary depression may follow a success. After the peak has been reached you are left exhausted, or you start to worry about what you will do next.

15. Indecision is another cause of depression. This occurs when you are caught between one decision or another, one attitude or another; you can't make up your mind. You become depressed.

The causes of depression are many. You must be able to recognize them and then move to do something about them. Don't take depression lightly. It is serious and can radically affect your life. It isn't so much what happens to you that counts, but how you respond to what happens.

KEYS TO WINNING OVER DEPRESSION

To properly win over depression you must be able to respond positively to circumstances and things which may cause depression. If you can do this, your depression won't last as long or be as harmful as it could be otherwise.

I believe the following suggestions will help you win over depression.

1. Don't be afraid or ashamed to acknowledge that you are depressed. It happens to all of us at one time or another. Take a few minutes to answer *why* you are depressed.

2. Never forget that God will help you win over

depression. Invite Him into the specific situation that is depressing you. He cares.

3. Admit your weakness to God; pray specifically about it. Never forget that he answers prayer (James 1:3-7).

4. Change your routine. Take a vacation. Get another job. Rest awhile. Read Mark 6:31 and go and do likewise.

5. Have a physical checkup. Ask your physician about your medication if you suspect it as a contributor to your depression.

6. Try to respond positively to circumstances on a daily basis. You are in control of your life.

7. If you are not involved in an exercise program, after you have your physician's approval, start one.

8. Use your creative imagination to win over depression. In your relaxed mood visualize your depression being removed, etc.

9. If you have been inactive, become active: do something daily; work on small successes; get involved with friends, family, work; entertain if possible; reach out to others; try giving yourself away.

10. Remember: "This too shall pass!"

11. Share your frustrations with a brother or sister in the church. We must bear one another's burdens (cf. Galatians 6:1, 2).

12. Learn some coping techniques by reading some good books on the subject of depression. Also, read the book of Proverbs.

13. Always remember that God loves you (cf John 3:16). You must love yourself.

14. Try to rid yourself of negative, self-defeating beliefs (e.g., You are not ugly; there are other jobs, etc.).

15. Try not to make any major decisions when you are depressed. For example many people decide to end their marriage when they are depressed.

16. Don't drag on and on with discussions about your depression. Prolonged discussion of your feelings intensifies them. You get what you say!

17. Don't blame others for your depression. You are responsible for what you think.

18. Never try to escape from reality by using drugs or alcohol. They only make things worse.

19. Set some realistic goals for your life. This keeps you on a positive track.

20. Don't take lightly any thoughts that you may have about killing yourself. This is a danger signal. Tell someone about your feelings. List all your reasons for living. See a professional counselor.

21. Remember "our sufficiency is of God" (II Corinthians 3:5).

22. Confess all your sins and faults to God (I John 1:7-9).

23. Meditate on God's word (Psalm 119:97; John 8:32).

There are many resources available for the Christian to use in his quest to win over depression. Today, medicine, psychology and God's word can help almost everyone who becomes depressed. The key is to use these resources.

CONCLUSION

There are many things that bring us to despair and on into states of depression. God doesn't want us to be robbed of joy and peace through depression. This is why He helps us win over it. No matter how dark the clouds may be, Jesus is always by our side. He understands. He cares. He said, "Come unto me, all ye that labour and are heavy laden, and I will give you rest" (Matthew 11:28).

You often can't control depression and other emotional problems that come into your life. But the good news is: you don't have to let them stay in your life and grow into worse problems. With God's help you can stop their growth. You can win over depression. The choice is yours. The time to begin is now.

FOR THOUGHT AND DISCUSSION

1. Why is depression an emotion we must win over?
2. Give an illustration of depression.
3. Do you often get depressed? Do you know someone who does? Discuss.
4. Is depression an isolated American problem?
5. What are some major contributors in our day to depression?
6. Discuss the definition of depression.
7. How can a person know if he/she is depressed?
8. Why are some cases of depression more serious than others?
9. Is depression a sin? Discuss.
10. Can you think of additional Bible examples of depression?
11. How can music help depression? Can it also cause depression?
12. T or F. Only the spiritually weak get depressed?
13. Discuss some major causes of depression.
14. How do you plan to use this lesson?
15. Discuss the keys to winning over depression.

CHAPTER THIRTEEN

WINNING OVER LOW SELF-ESTEEM

"Then God said, Let us make man in our image, in our likeness . . . So God created man in his own image, in the image of God he created him; male and female . . . God saw all that he made, and it was very good . . ."

(Genesis 1:26, 27, 31)

INTRODUCTION

Wayne had not attended church services for several weeks. In his words, here is his reason for quiting: "The church doesn't need me. I just don't fit in down there . . . I'm not important."

In talking to fourteen-year-old, Harold, about his conduct problem in school, he replied, "I guess you could say that I am a born loser."

George was asked to make a short talk to a group of men in church. In rejecting the invitation, he said, "I can't talk before the group because I don't have anything worth listening to."

Suzy was invited to serve as a hostess in a wedding reception. She declined because, to quote her words, "I have two left hands and would make a mess of things."

Little Timmy was asked by his father to join a group of children in a game of baseball. Timmy struck out his first time at bat, and refused to play anymore. In spite of his dad's encouragement, he refused to play. In an upset tone, he shouted at his father, "There is no use for me to try. I can't hit the ball. I know I will strike out again!"

These five illustrations all have one thing in common. They are examples from every day life of persons expressing low self-esteem. Low self-esteem is a very common feeling among people. It is an emotion that Christians must properly win over.

It is hard to imagine that 95 percent of all people in our society have a problem with low self-esteem, which is manifested in feelings of inferiority. Dr. Maxwell Maltz, in his book *Psycho-Cybernetics*, wrote, "At least 95% of the people have their lives blighted by feelings of inferiority to some extent, and to millions this same feeling of inferiority is a serious handicap to success and happiness."

Everyone has an opinion of himself. Many times it is expressed by such statements as, "Oh, that's just the way I am"; "When I get mad you had better stay out of my way. I can't control myself"; "I can't stand to see myself in a mirror. I'm so ugly"; or some other put-down expression.

In this lesson we want to learn how to win over low self-esteem.

WHAT IS SELF-ESTEEM?

Self-esteem relates to your self-identity. It deals with these three questions: (1) *who am I?* (2) *what am I?* (3) *why am I?* For example you may refer to "who am I" by giving your name or some other mark of indentification. When you say "I am a Christian" you are referring to what you are. When you state, "I work hard to provide a living for my family," you give an answer to "why am I?"

There are two related words that need to be clarified in order to get a clear picture of self-esteem. The first word is *self-image*. Self-image is a term that describes how I see myself. If I think of myself as short and ugly this is my self-image. The second word is *self-confidence*. Self-confidence refers to my belief in my ability. If you challenge me to fly an airplane, I have no self-confidence because I know I can't pilot a plane. This doesn't mean that I have a problem with low self-esteem; only a problem with confidence.

Real self-esteem is the *value* you place upon yourself as a person. This is why a person may have self-confidence and not have self-esteem at the same time. For example, Sam is confident in his ability to drive a truck, but he thinks of himself as an "odd ball" or "misfit" in company politics. Self-esteem is how you feel about yourself within the chambers of your mind. It is how you feel when you are alone or in a crowd. *Worth* is another word that defines self-esteem. High self-esteem comes from feeling lovable and worthwhile. It evolves from many positive life experiences. Conversely, low self-esteem comes from negative conclusions we draw about ourselves. Distortion is the thief that robs you of self-esteem.

Dr. David D. Burns, in his book *Feeling Good*, says, "Self-esteem is the capacity to experience maximal self-love and joy whether or not you are successful at any point in your life" (pp. 229, 230). Burns further states, "Self-esteem can be defined as the state that exists when you are not arbitrarily haranguis and abusing yourself but choose to fight back against those automatic thoughts with meaningful rational response" (p. 293).

Many Christians have such low self-esteem that they have adopted as their theme song a line from the hymn which says, "Would He devote that sacred head for such a worm as I?" It's a challenge for children of God to develop proper self-esteem when our songs remind us of how inferior we are. People value themselves to the degree that they have been valued. We let others provide the mirrors that determine our self-image and value. We go through life drawing conclusions about ourselves as we compare ourselves with others. To raise your self-esteem you must not let others determine your worth. This is a job reserved for God.

What is self-esteem? It is the VALUE you place upon yourself as a person.

CONSEQUENCES OF LOW SELF-ESTEEM

Because of the decision to treat yourself with low

self-esteem, you have set yourself up to become the victim of many possible consequences that aren't good. A list of the results of low self-esteem is almost endless. Some of the more serious ones are as follows:

1. A negative vocabulary filled with such expressions as: "I'm no good"; "I can't ever do anything right"; "I'm a dummy"; etc. This kind of self-talk will never raise your self-esteem.

2. A lack of inner peace and comfort.

3. Collecting of all kinds of *rewards* to prove one's worth.

4. Failure to be involved with others. Being a loner.

5. Constant self-criticism and rejection of self.

6. Constantly trying to impress everyone.

7. Always giving negative reaction to compliments. When told the jacket she is wearing is very pretty, she may react, "Oh, this old thing . . ."

8. Bragging and self-conceit. He will let you know he is the greatest.

9. Always trying to outdo the other person.

10. Constantly talking about something he has done.

11. Children misbehave. Adults violate social standards or laws of the land.

12. Self-indulgence; overeating, etc.

13. Too much emphasis on being confident; e.g., rough handshake; loud laugh, etc.

14. Afraid of anyone seeing her as she really is. Wears a mask to hide her feelings of worthlessness.

15. Building of defenses around weaknesses.

16. A drive for power, superiority, or control over others.

17. Always complaining or arguing.

18. Low self-esteem causes a person to place impossible demands upon himself. This is why he is never able to succeed, which in turn causes more low self-esteem.

19. A feeling of helplessness or inability to overcome faults.

20. Anger, guilt, resentment and a host of other problems arise from low self-esteem.

When a person places a low value upon himself, virtually every emotion, thought and attitude is affected. Low self-esteem robs a person of his pride in being a member of the human family. A person who has lost his dignity is like a ship without a compass: his life goes in one direction and then another trying to reach the shores of happiness. Until he gets his life right with God, and understands who he really is, there will never be an end to his pseudo attempts to prove his worth. Almost every sin, at one point or another, is a manifestation of low self-esteem. How can a person who feels good about himself rebel against the God who created him in His image? Read James 1:13-17 for the answer.

CAUSES OF LOW SELF-ESTEEM

Like all other emotions, self-esteem occurs within the mind. It is an attitude we hold relative to our value as a person. Self-esteem is the result of many experiences in life, especially in childhood. Feelings of inferiority begin early in life as parents program their children with all kinds of value labels. It is not the occasional rebuke or criticism that damages the child's self-esteem. It is the constant criticism, rejection, scolding, shaming and insulting by parents that produce feelings of low self-esteem. When a child grows up without praise, encouragement, compliments, affectionate embraces, and emotional support, he arrives at adulthood with low self-esteem.

When the child starts to school he is confronted with an additional list of challenges to his self-esteem. His performance becomes the test of his worth. How he runs, plays ball, jumps, and a host of other activities determine how others will think about him. He is always wondering: "Do I perform well enough to be chosen or accepted?" "I can play as well as Charlie, why don't they choose me?" Add to this the fact that his clothes also determine his worth and you can easily see why he feels down on himself.

As the child moves into adolescence he becomes even more aware of status labels. He has learned that some people are more important than others. Some are shy or withdrawn, others never seem to fit in. Labels like "dumb," "four-eyes," "clod," "air-head," and a host of others are given by peers as symbols of worth and rejection. His deep desire is to be accepted. He longs to be popular and admired. He desires to be the greatest. Some never learn that neither appearance, performance, nor status determines their value as a person.

As we move through life we become more and more indoctrinated with the worldly philosophy that our worth is determined by what we have achieved in life. There is nothing wrong with feeling good about accomplishments. The challenge is not to let them become the standards that determine our worth. If your achievements determine your value, what will you do when you lose your job, become ill, retire, have a business reversal, etc.? You will become depressed.

Religion has, in many cases, contributed to feelings of low self-esteem. For example, the denominational doctrine which states that man is born totally depraved, robs man of his sense of self-worth. He must go through life hoping that God will arbitrarily choose to save him. It is true that sin is bad, and God hates it. But it is also true that God loves the sinner (cf. John 3:16). Man must not view himself as a *worm*. Jesus didn't die for worms. He died for human beings created in God's image. The gospel is a message of good news.

Your self-esteem, in the final analysis, is the result of what you choose to think and believe about yourself. You choose to feel inferior, or you choose to feel good about yourself. No other person has the power to control your feelings. You don't have to reject yourself, or depreciate yourself because of some failure or inability in your life. You are an okay person. Perfection is not the problem. Inner feelings of worthwhileness and goodness are the real issues you must face and win over as you battle for self-esteem. Never forget that just because you feel inferior, it doesn't mean that you are inferior.

THE BIBLE AND SELF-ESTEEM

Through the years men have had a problem with low self-esteem. Thus, contrary to the thinking of some, it didn't originate in the twentieth century. It should be noted that God's word presents life as it is. It doesn't try to cover up the weaknesses of its heros. There are many accounts of outstanding leaders wrestling with a low estimate of themselves and their abilities.

1. When God called Moses to become a leader of His people, he flinched and offered a number of excuses for not being ready to respond (Read Exodus 3:8-11; 4:10-17). For some reason Moses lacked self-confidence.

2. Gideon was viewed by God as a mighty man of valour (Judges 6:12). When God called him for a mighty

mission, however, he tried to get out of it by claiming he came from a poor family (Judges 6:15). He felt inadequate for the job.

3. Jeremiah, one of the great prophets of God, replied to Jehovah's initial call with these words, ". . . Ah, Lord God! behold, I cannot speak: for I am a child" (Jere. 1:6). Jeremiah is expressing a low estimate of his worth as a servant of God.

4. When Amaziah asked Amos not to prophesy anymore, he replied, ". . . I was not a prophet, neither was I a prophet's son; but I was a herdsman, and a gatherer of sycamore fruit" (Amos 7:14).

Regardless of our interpretation of the above verses, one thing is obvious. These men of God reflected upon their stations and abilities in life. At least three of them tried to use them to justify their rejection of God's call. And, yet, God thought so much of them that He called them to do great works. God doesn't value His creation as men value it. He sees the worth of EVERY person.

God's word provides us with a sound basis for self-esteem. It is bound up in this truth: *You are created in the image of God, and this image is good* (cf. Genesis 1: 26, 27). Ethel Waters was right when she said, "God don't make no junk." Man stands at the height of creation. He is the only being (or thing) created in the image of God. Take some time and think about the implications of this great truth.

Another reason for proper self-esteem is the fact that God loves you. This love motivated Him to give His Son for your salvation (cf. John 3:16; Romans 5:6-10).

A third truth that should raise your self-esteem is the price Christ paid for your redemption. Everyone agrees that the value of a thing is determined by what it cost. Peter reminds us of our worth when he writes, "Forasmuch as ye know that ye were not redeemed with corruptible things, as silver and gold, from your vain conversation received by traditions from your fathers; but with the precious blood of Christ, as of a lamb without blemish and without spot" (I Peter 1:18, 19; cf. Revelation 1:5; Acts 20:28). You are so valuable that nothing but the blood of Christ can atone for your soul (cf. Mark 8:36-38).

James raises our self-esteem by reminding us that we are "heirs of the kingdom" (James 2:5). This means that we are co-heirs with Christ, Who is our elder brother. There are no rejects or inferior children in God's family. As Christians we are going to receive an inheritance from our Father (cf. I Peter 1:2-5; Romans 8:17).

Paul reminded the Corinthian brethren that every member of the church was very important. He wrote, "Now ye are the body of Christ, and members in particular" (I Corinthians 12:27; also read 12:12-31). Thus, every Christian is a VIP. You have something to contribute to the church that no other member can contribute; this is why you are essential to the progress of the church.

Jesus tells us through the pen of John, that God so esteems His saints, that: "To him that overcometh will I grant to sit with me in my throne, even as I also overcame, and am set down with my Father in His throne" (Revelation 3:21). Can you visualize yourself enjoying this promise of God? This should help you elevate your self-esteem.

Do you feel good about yourself? God has placed a high value upon you as a person created in His image. He has invested the blood of His Son to secure your eternal redemption. This, without a doubt, establishes your worth. Meditate on these truths.

SELF-LOVE

If you want to raise your low self-esteem, you must develop a healthy self-love. Jesus said, "Thou shalt love thy neighbor as thyself" (Matthew 19:19). Paul wrote, "So ought men to love their wives as their own bodies. He that loveth his wife loveth himself" (Ephesians 5:28). It's okay to have love for yourself as long as it is not selfish or ego centered. Egomania is not approved by God.

The phrase, "The Greeks had a word for it," is certainly true in the area of love. In English, basically only one word expresses the emotion called love. The Greeks, however, had several words to express different meanings. We translate them all with the English word love. The English thinking mind is free to define love as he chooses. The average person would probably define it as a "warm emotional feeling." Therefore, when we turn and read Jesus' command to love our enemies, we become frustrated, wondering how we can have a "warm emotional feeling" toward our enemy. This problem is solved, however, when we define the particular Greek word which was used by Jesus.

When the Greeks wanted to express tender affection, they used the word *phileo*. Jesus used this word in describing the Father's affection for Him (cf. John 3:35). Brotherly love was expressed by the word *philadelphos* (cf. Romans 12:10; I Peter 1:22).

There was also the *agape* form of love. This type of love isn't based upon the emotions. It is a decision of the will to put the other person's well being first. It evokes positive action in spite of how one feels. *Agape* regards the welfare of another, as well as one's own welfare. Nothing could be better for your welfare than to raise your level of self-esteem.

Self-love, when properly understood, should motivate a person to prepare his soul for its eternal destiny. The "worse self" must be exchanged for a better self. This is what Jesus taught with regard to a "new birth of water and Spirit" (cf. John 3:1-5).

Self-love is based upon your uniqueness and value as a person created in God's image. If you ever doubt you are loved, turn to the Gospels and read the account of how Christ suffered for you on the cross. May this motivate you to raise your self-esteem as a person created in God's image.

KEYS TO WINNING

Changing low self-esteem won't occur in a day or two. It will take time, a plan, dedication and work. As part of your plan for winning over low self-esteem, study and use the following points.

1. Don't freely criticize yourself. Confront this negative attitude and habit when it pops into your mind.

2. Take a sheet of paper and answer this question: What does it mean to be created in God's image?

3. Reorganize your basic beliefs about yourself. This will take self-examination and specific targets.

4. Don't let the threat of change stop you. Think of how you will feel after your self-esteem improves.

5. Try to discover why you have low self-esteem. Be honest with yourself.

6. Feed your self-esteem. Think good thoughts about yourself.

7. Don't try to be too analytical of everything that happens, or of every remark a person makes about you.

8. Through visualization see yourself removing all negative labels from yourself. Place a label that states, "I am created in God's image."

9. Don't worry about the past or future. Trust God (Matthew 6:25-35).

10. Dwell on Biblical truths about your worth. Accept God's estimate of your worth.

11. Remember that your worth is not determined by your successes or approvals in life.

12. Other than God, don't let anyone else take charge of your life. You are in control of your thoughts (cf. Proverbs 23:7).

13. Don't be impatient or too hard on yourself. God is not finished with you.

14. Make a list of all your positive qualities. If you doubt having them, you have fallen victim to negative thinking, the major enemy to self-esteem.

15. Eliminate or try to avoid those situations which contribute to your low self-esteem.

16. Count your blessings and rejoice over all the good things God is doing in your life.

17. Do something. Take a walk. Help a person in need. Try giving instead of getting.

CONCLUSION

You are the product of your past and your present thinking. Try as you may, you cannot deny it or completely break away from it. The challenge, therefore, is to recognize this and invite God to help you develop proper self-esteem. Through Biblical direction you can win over negative self-esteem. Also, be sure to ask yourself if you are contributing to another person's low self-esteem by your remarks and attitude toward that person.

Your life will be better if you let God help you develop your self-esteem. Today is the day to begin!

FOR THOUGHT AND DISCUSSION

1. Is low self-esteem a problem in the church?
2. Do you have a problem with low self-esteem?
3. Define self-esteem.
4. How does self-image relate to self-esteem?
5. How does worth relate to self-esteem?
6. How does negative thinking relate to self-esteem?
7. What are some major consequences of low self-esteem?
8. What are some signs of low self-esteem?
9. How does low self-esteem relate to sin?
10. Where does self-esteem occur?
11. How early do we start developing our self-esteem?
12. Discuss Genesis 1:26, 27.
13. Discuss Bible examples of low self-esteem.
14. Discuss self-love and its relationship to self-esteem.
15. How do you plan to use this lesson in your daily life?

BIBLIOGRAPHY

Adams, Jay E. *The Christian Counselor's Manual.* Grand Rapids, Mich. Baker Book House, 1973.

Allport, G. *Patterns And Growth In Personality.* Rinehart and Winston, 1961.

Bailey, Covert. *Fit or Fat.* Houghton Mifflin Co , New York. Boston, Mass., 1977.

Burns, David D. *Feeling Good.* New York. William Morrow and Co., 1980.

Cabot, Richard. *What Men Live By.*

Collins, Gary R. *Christian Counseling.* Waco, Tx. Word Books, 1980.

Cooped, L. *The Rhetoric of Aristotle.* New York. D. Appleton-Century, 1932.

Cooper, Kenneth H. *The New Aerobics.* New York. Bantam Books, 1970.

Donsbach, Kurt. *Stress.* International Institute of Natural Health Science. Huntington Beach, Ca., 1981.

Dyer, Wayne. *Your Erroneous Zones.* New York. Avon Books, 1976.

Emery, Gary. *A New Beginning.* New York. Simon and Schuster, 1981.

Friedman, Meyer and Roseman, H. Ray. *Type A Behavior And Your Heart.* Connecticut. Fawcett Crest Book, 1974.

Guralnik, David B. (Editor). *Webster's New World Dictionary.* Nashville. The Southwestern Co., 1964.

Haldane, Bernard. *How To Make Success A Habit.* New York. Warner Books, 1975.

Hansel, Tim. *When I Relax I Feel Guilty.* Elgin, IL, David C. Cook Publishing Co., 1979.

Harriman, P. L. *Dictionary of Psychology.* New York. Philosophical Library, 1947.

Hill, Napoleon. *Think And Grow Rich Action Pack.* New York. Hawthorn Books, Inc., 1972.

Hyder, O. Quentin. *Shape Up.* N. J., Fleming H. Revell, 1979.

Keyser, Leander. *Oxford Dictionary of English Etymology.* Burlington, Vt. The Lutheran Board, 1928.

Maltz, Maxwell. *Psycho-Cybernetics.* New York. Pocket Books, Inc., 1966.

Minnick, Wayne C. *The Art of Persuasion, 2nd Ed.* Boston. Haughton Mifflin, 1968.

Moody, Raymond A. *Laugh After Laugh.* Jacksonville, Fl. Headwater Press, 1978.

Mowrer, Hobart O. *The Crisis of Psychiatry and Religion.* Princeton. Van Nostrand, 1961.

MacDonald, M. A. *Chambers Etymological English Dictionary.* London. W. R. Chambers, LTD.

McMillen, I. S. *None Of These Diseases.* N. J., Spire Book: Revell Co., 1967.

McQuade, Walter and Aikman, Ann. *Stress.* New York. Bantam Books, 1974.

Narramore, Clyde M. *Encyclopedia of Psychological Problems.* Grand Rapids, Mich. Zondervan, 1976.

Oyle, Irving. *The Healing Mind.* Celestial Arts. Millbrae, CA, 1975.

Pritikin, Nathan. *The Pritikin Permanent Weight-Loss Manual.* New York. Bantam Books, 1981.

Selye, Hans. *The Stress of Life.* New York. McGraw-Hill Book Co., 1976.

Simonton, Carl O., Matthew-Simonton, Stephanie, and Creighton, James L. *Getting Well Again.* New York. Bantam Books, 1978.

Tulloh, Bruce. *Natural Fitness.* London. Arrow Books. 1976.

Turner, J. J. *Positive Christian Living.* West Monroe, La. Self-Improvement Institute, 1979.

Vine, E. W. *An Expository Dictionary of New Testament Words.* N. J., Fleming H. Revell Co., 1966 (edition).

Unger, Merrel. *Bible Dictionary.* Chicago, Ill. Moody Press, 1957.

Other Helpful Books By:

J. J. Turner

DOCTRINE OF THE GODHEAD

This study of the Father, Son, and Holy Spirit by J.J. Turner and Edward P. Myers covers subjects such as The Attributes of God, The Triune Godhead, The Nature of God, and The Incarnation of Jesus. The Holy Spirit of God, of Today, and in the Testaments is also discussed.

POSITIVE CHRISTIAN LIVING

This book sets forth some core truths that are designed to help you move ahead in daily positive Christian living. The material in this book has been used effectively in positive spiritual attitude seminars across the nation. The key is to become a positive Christian in your daily living.

HOW TO TURN YOUR DREAMS INTO REALITIES

This self-improvement book seeks to motivate you to go to work on making your dreams a reality. Some of the chapter titles are: "Whatever Happened To All The Great Things You Were Going To Do?", "It's Not Too Late," "Find A Way Or Make One," "30 Mistakes On The Road To Success," and "Unleashing Your Potential."

WINNING THROUGH A POSITIVE SPIRITUAL ATTITUDE

This book sets forth a sound biblical approach to being successful in ALL areas of life. It is fast becoming a best seller in the brotherhood as it is being used in special classes, as well as ladies Bible classes.

THE BOOK OF JAMES

This practical book is designed to give an understandable exegesis of the text with application for people of today.

GOD'S WAY TO THE TOP

We have a lot of advice today on how to get to the top, but it should be remembered that God also has some information on how to succeed and get to the top. This book is about that advice.

These books may be ordered from

Quality Publications
P.O. Box 1060
Abilene, Texas 79604

or your favorite bookstore.